GOOD sex

Also by Catherine M. Roach

Happily Ever After: The Romance Story in Popular Culture

Mother/Nature: Popular Culture and Environmental Ethics

Stripping, Sex, and Popular Culture

GOOD
sex

Transforming America through the New Gender and Sexual Revolution

Catherine M. Roach, PhD

INDIANA UNIVERSITY PRESS

This book is a publication of

Indiana University Press
Office of Scholarly Publishing
Herman B Wells Library 350
1320 East 10th Street
Bloomington, Indiana 47405 USA

iupress.org

Manufactured in the United States of America

First printing 2022

Cataloging information is available from the Library of Congress.

ISBN 978-0-253-06468-4 (hardback)
ISBN 978-0-253-06469-1 (paperback)
ISBN 978-0-253-06470-7 (ebook)

To the next generation:

My sons, Benjamin and Nathaniel,
and all their friends throughout the years.
You lead us forward.

And my students, especially to C.
Your stories and your vision of a better future led me to this project.

CONTENTS

Manisexto #1

POSITIVE SEXUALITY   13

Sexuality Is a Normal, Healthy, and Pleasurable Aspect of Being Human

Manisexto #2

EQUITY AND INCLUSION   55

Gender and Sexual Identities Are Diverse—and That's Okay

Manisexto #5

SHARED PLEAJURE   177

Good Sex Is Mutually Pleasurable and Respectful

You'll hear from the undergraduates in my Sexuality & Society course in the quotations throughout the book, highlighted by this student graphic. The responses, all presented here anonymously, come from the students' coursework material and with their full permission to be included in the book.

A portion of the sales proceeds from *Good Sex* goes to support student programming at the University of Alabama for equity and inclusion events.

PREFACE

Every term, I ask the university students in my Sexuality & Society course what they think about the pressures and possibilities around gender and sexuality these days. Here's a typical response:

> "Things are really different from before, from how my parents' generation dealt with sex and gender. You can be more yourself now, with more choices, but a lot of people still get hurt. A lot's gotten better, but not everything. It's up to us now."

> You'll hear from the undergraduates in my Sexuality & Society course in the quotations throughout the book, highlighted by this student graphic. The responses, all presented here anonymously, come from the students' coursework material and with their full permission to be included in the book.

I wrote this book because of this dual sense that "things are really different from before" and "it's up to us now." I saw signs of a hopeful, although still incomplete, revolution unfolding among my students and echoing far beyond them, throughout the culture as a whole. The book pulls this vision into focus. For the generation now coming of age, how they think about and experience sex and gender have changed. A coherent new set of understandings, gaining ground across all age demographics, is becoming everyday reality for the American public.

While some critics think this cultural transformation means the country has tumbled down a slippery slope and lost its way in a landscape of anything goes, I am here to argue the opposite. This twenty-first-century shift upholds core American principles of equality, freedom, happiness, and personal responsibility. It has the potential to resolve enduring injustices and contradictions around gender and sexuality. It strengthens civil society. It is changing America for the better.

This book draws deeply on the space of the classroom and offers a window into its lively discussions. It is chock full of comments from the hundreds of students who've passed through the course over the years. I deliberately minimize my use of secondary sources written by academic experts (although you'll find these recommendations for further reading in the back). Instead, I highlight the students' own ideas, expressed in their own words, as the primary sources that make and illustrate many of the book's arguments. These young people are the "experts" on this moment of America at a turning point, since their generation is the one riding and building this wave into the future. The book is a type of dialogue between me and these students. Our discussion intertwines across the pages, in an experiment with form.

I invite the reader to join in this encounter. As in the college classroom where my students and I collaboratively map out these changing cultural patterns, I want readers to think and argue along with me. My goal is to structure a fair-minded conversation that deepens awareness about the commitments and implications of the new gender and sexual revolution: where we are headed and why it's a good thing. We're not going to agree on everything, but for the sake of such a crucial topic, there's a whole lot we should be talking about. How to understand and navigate today's new landscape. How to think critically about its challenges and potential.

Buckle in. Here comes an accessible guidebook to chart the changing terrain of gender and sexuality.

GOOD
sex

FOREPLAY

Introducing the Manisexto

A Manifesto for the New Gender and Sexual Revolution

A cultural revolution unfolds in America.

It emerges from #MeToo activism against sexual misconduct, media campaigns around body positivity, and the increased visibility of people from across the gender and sexuality spectrum. These varied developments stand at the leading edge of a broad shift happening across America and the globe. Together, they herald a welcome revolution for the twenty-first century and a new vision of sexual and gender well-being.

In the popular culture and public sphere, a recent wave of discussion about sex and gender has grabbed mainstream attention. Back in 2014, *Time* magazine proclaimed America at a transgender tipping point, shortly after then vice president Joe Biden endorsed transgender rights as a crucial civil rights issue. Actress and social justice advocate Laverne Cox (a native of my state of Alabama) graced that *Time* cover, signaling the rise of transgender issues to celebrity status. In 2015, the US Supreme Court decided in support of same-sex marriage. Around the same time, the percentage of married households in the US hit a historic low. Delayed marriage, serial relationships, and the singledom movement with its vision of sexy spinsterhood offered options to traditional patterns of matrimony. Starting in 2017, a pink-pussy-hat surge of female energy fueled the #MeToo move-

In 2015, the US Supreme Court decided in support of same-sex marriage.

After the 2020 Supreme Court ruling that guaranteed civil rights against workplace discrimination, the *New York Times* commented, "The decision is the strongest evidence yet of how fundamentally, rapidly and, to some degree, unpredictably American views about gay and transgender people have changed across the ideological spectrum in less than 20 years."

ment against previously tolerated or hushed-up sexual wrongdoing. Calls of "Enough is enough!" began to upend old power dynamics. The year 2020 saw another landmark Supreme Court case, this one declaring it unconstitutional for companies to fire employees simply because they are lesbian, gay, bisexual, or transgender. All along, ever-growing media representation continued to deepen public awareness of diversity: of asexual orien-

Actress, producer, and prominent equal rights advocate Laverne Cox posing at a Women's March event.

tations that sidestep the hubbub of desire, of polyamory and other forms of consensual nonmonogamy, of intersex conditions and nonbinary gender identities that call into question the absoluteness of the male-female divide.

The United States, of course, is not alone in these developments. It's beyond our scope to trace the global context of these trends, except to note that the broad shift is happening internationally if unevenly, particularly in North and South America, Australia, and Europe. To give just one indication, as of 2022 marriage equality for same-sex couples exists in thirty-one countries worldwide (up from zero before 2000). The list grows every year.

While a puritanical past shapes America, the twenty-first century has ushered in huge changes, fast. All these transformations, disparate yet interrelated, result in greater cultural acceptance and legal protection for diversity in gender expression and romance. A brave new world opens before us: we live in an era of a new gender and sexual revolution.

A person who is *transgender* has a sense of their internal gender identity that differs from the male or female biological sex they were assigned at birth. They may use hormone therapy and sometimes surgery to transition away from their birth sex. A person who is *cisgender*—from the Latin prefix *cis*—meaning "this side of"—feels that their birth sex aligns well with their gender identity; they grow up comfortably identifying as the girl/woman or boy/man that parents and medical professionals proclaimed them to be at birth. Note that these terms both refer to an identity (whether one identifies as male, female, or nonbinary) and are not about sexual desire.

This moment builds on the earlier sex-positive revolution of the 1960s and early '70s, fueled by that era's counterculture movement and widespread availability of reliable contraceptives. But it adds fresh emphasis on broader inclusion. We increasingly talk about personal identity as shaped through the overlapping intersection of gender and sexuality, as well as categories of race, ethnicity, socioeconomic class, body size and shape, age, dis/ability status, and more. (Academics term this overlap of aspects of identity *intersectionality*.) This next-generation revolution makes a deeper commitment to sexual justice through a hard line against sexual misconduct and through informed, affirma-

Starting in 2017, a pink-pussy-hat surge of female energy fueled the #MeToo movement and protest marches across the country.

tive consent. It provides wider freedom from the mandatory gender binary of masculinity or femininity. It celebrates body positivity. And it works to reduce the stigma of slut-shaming and to celebrate "cliteracy" (yup, we're going to talk about closing the orgasm gap). These transformational shifts are happening through online means unimaginable fifty, or even ten, years ago: digital platforms and social media where people share personal stories to create community and empower activism.

People are taking part in this new cultural dialogue, reported and debated through news outlets, magazines, websites, Twitter feeds, and at workplace watercoolers. Mirroring this public conversation is recent research from the fields of sexuality and gender studies. From journalist Peggy Orenstein's best-selling *Girls & Sex* (2016) and its follow-up *Boys & Sex* (2020) to sociologist Barbara Risman's

In 2016, the Merriam-Webster dictionary added the words *cisgender, gender-fluid, gender-queer,* and *transphobia*. In 2020, Dictionary.com added *gender-inclusive, trans+,* and *MeToo*.

In 2020, the American Dialect Society chose *they* used as a gender-neutral singular pronoun as its "Word of the Decade," after previously deeming it their "Word of the Year" in 2015, in their annual vote for the standout expression most indicative of North America's social and cultural landscape. I adopt this common practice in this book and use *they* (and *them/their*) in the singular form instead of *he* or *she* (*his* or *her*)—as in "Each person gets to decide what happens to their body," as opposed to "Each person gets to decide what happens to his or her body."

Where the Millennials Will Take Us: A New Generation Wrestles with the Gender Structure (2018), academic writers and cultural observers alike are framing their analyses in terms of a "new landscape" of sex and gender emerging in America. *National Geographic* devoted a special issue of their magazine (2017) and a documentary film to the new "gender revolution." "The world is indeed at a moment of Gender Vertigo," writes Risman, citing American society's ever-closer move "toward a post-gender society." And college-culture expert Donna Freitas declares in *Consent on Campus* (2018) that "we have arrived at a pivotal moment with regard to rape culture, sexual harassment, and sexual assault."

As a site of research tracing this shifting landscape, the American college plays a central role. Universities are harbingers of groundbreaking ideas. What professors lecture about, campus activists organize around, and students live out all give evidence of where the country is going. Coast to coast, universities are leading national conversations about sexual justice but also struggling to ensure such gender equity and sexual well-being for their young people. In 2014, the California state legislature enacted a legal standard of "active and affirmative consent" aimed at decreasing college sexual assault amid the campus party scene. At that time, high-profile federal investigations of sexually hostile environments at top schools such as Harvard and Princeton were ongoing. At my school, the University of Alabama, as at many others, student activists led "Walks of Shame" and "Take

All-genders restroom sign.

Universities are incubators for innovative ideas and cultural trends.

Back the Night" rallies to combat sexual misconduct and end a culture of silence and slut-shaming. We have a column for preferred pronouns on our class enrollment lists, enabling students to indicate "she," "he," or "they." We host an annual State of the Queer Union panel and Lavender Graduation for the LGBTQ community. Students run active chapters of reproductive justice and gender equity groups.

Big picture? The cultural mood has altered. All these changes have us at a turning point, with more support than ever before for diversity and equity. American society is working out and reaching toward a bold new vision of sexuality and gender.

> "People should be able to love and find happiness in any way that they can, and labels or society should not be able to have the power to stop them."

The vision, however, remains incomplete. As a society, we haven't reached full consensus or agreement. The standard conventions for gender and relationships—what it means to be a woman or a man, what "masculine" and "feminine" are supposed to look like, how we are expected to pair off romantically—are loosening and changing, but society still tends to privilege traditional story lines about gender and partnering up. Alongside progress in human rights such as the 2015 recognition of marriage equality, backlash abounds. Homophobia still exists, not only as occasional slurs

"According to a 2019 study by the Southern Poverty Law Center, the number of hate groups active in the US hit its highest level in two decades, with the most growth among white nationalist organizations but including groups hostile to lesbian, gay, and transgender people."

tossed around in ignorant bullying, but as systematic discrimination and even as targeted violence that kills. Here in Alabama, a pair of opposing rallies took place on the steps of our state supreme court in Montgomery. One side supported last-ditch efforts to prevent same-sex couples from obtaining marriage licenses, and the other side, rainbow flags happily waving, made the point that the fight had already been lost. As presidential administrations and state legislatures flip back and forth across partisan divides, laws and directives—regarding, for example, transgender military service or restroom access—pass and are then retracted or legislated anew.

Risman, in her sociological study, asks, "How can we understand simultaneous advancements in gender and sexuality equity and sometimes what seems to be radical steps backward? . . . Is the gender revolution ongoing?" To some degree, backlash is inevitable. Change stirs things up; it upends power dynamics, flattens previous hierarchies, and questions unearned privilege that worked to the advantage of certain groups. As a result, confusion, misinformation, anger, and bigotry can remain rife. Such reactions range from well-intentioned uncertainty to the crimes of full-fledged hate groups. The upshot? At no time in American history have traditional sexual and gender norms been so up for grabs and open to alternatives—yet still so unsettled and under dispute.

Many people think this openness is a wonderful thing. I am one of them. Maybe you, too, are happy with these changes and enjoying new forms of freedom and expression. But you might also be struggling with how to create enough safe space to be true to yourself. Maybe these new developments don't feel like more freedom or protection at all. Maybe just getting through the day still feels like an exhausting and dangerous effort, without having to lie and pretend and worry whether you'll be sneered at, fired, or beat up simply for being different. The pace of change may seem far too slow.

For others, the pace is far too fast. Maybe all this change feels like too much, too different from the tried-and-true. It's not what you grew up with, not what you learned from your parents, religion, school, or hometown. Maybe you feel blamed or under scrutiny now yourself, simply because the old norms still suit you fine and you're baffled by the new terminology: *pansexual, they/them pronouns, nonbinary*? At a sidewalk café, I overheard a woman talking to friends: "My stepdaughter just came out as polyamorous! Who comes up with these things?" she asked. Such concerns are understandable. These evolving norms introduce a learning curve. They require adjustments and can provoke anxiety. As individuals, we don't always know how to talk about and live out these shifts, how to respond in the public sphere or our family lives. It's a lot to process, and our online era speeds up change to a dizzying pace.

> "Some of our course readings made me feel like I am a bad person for being a white guy, as if my parents did something wrong by teaching me the traditional ideals of masculinity that I live by. But at the same time there were a lot of points about porn and sexual abuse that I think were well said."

In moments of pushback, it's easy to feel pessimistic about the direction of change, especially for those people caught in unjust realities of backlash. I am here to lay out reasons for believing that the long-term and big-picture view of history provides grounds for optimism. "The arc of the moral universe is long, but it bends toward justice," preached Martin Luther King Jr. (paraphrasing the nineteenth-century American minister and abolitionist Theodore Parker). He was arguing that civil rights progress is not only possible but—through committed activism—inevitable. Without being naive about ongoing injustices, we can be confident about the potential of the road ahead to increase freedom, possibility, and happiness.

In fact, the very backlash itself stands as evidence of the strength of the culture's shift. As feminist icon Gloria Steinem said in a recent interview with the *New York Times Magazine*, "We are at a point of a backlash because we are *winning.* . . . Now, most Americans agree with what social-justice movements have been saying [on issues such as gender equality and same-sex marriage]." The intensity of pushback is a sign of being on the defensive, a last gasp of resistance to the tides of change.

> "I believe that through time, things will get better. We have much more accepting people in my generation."

Here, then, are the five commitments of the new gender and sexual revolution that is working its way through the culture.

1. **Positive sexuality:** Sexuality is a normal, healthy, and pleasurable aspect of being human. People have the right to their sexual choices, as long as those choices are consensual and uphold partners' best interests. This vision of positive sexuality or "sex-positivity" is rooted in, but complicated by, the history of American attitudes toward sexuality.

2. **Equity and inclusion, normalizing diversity:** Sexual and gender identities take many forms. Because diversity is the norm, equity and inclusion are central values for a strong and democratic civil society.

3. **Body positivity:** No more shaming or bullying for not having the perfect body. The body acceptance movement redefines narrow cultural ideals of sexiness, beauty, and appropriate gender display. All bodies are good bodies. Looking and feeling good means inhabiting your body with joy.

4. **Consent:** Full consent is fundamental to all sexual activity. Meaningful consent arises out of egalitarian gender norms, based in new scripts about masculinity and femininity that rewrite gatekeeping, slut-shaming, double standards, and toxic "Man Box" rules.

5. **Shared pleasure:** Good sex is mutually respectful and pleasurable. It feels good for all partners. Time to close that orgasm gap! Time to learn about "cliteracy" and porn literacy. The twenty-first century features more inclusive gender scripts and narratives about egalitarian sex, love and romance, and healthy intimate relationships.

Together, these points constitute a five-step manifesto—a mani*sex*to, if you will. A manifesto is an open statement, a declaration of core principles and beliefs on an issue of public relevance. A manifesto propounds an argument, supports a cause, promotes a movement.

What I call the Manisexto is the essence of America's new gender and sexual revolution. It offers an analysis, at the levels of the individual and of society, about how our understanding of gender and sexuality is changing in a moment of transformational shift. The analysis of this shift grows from a foundation that unpacks the meaning of a positive attitude toward sexuality, builds with a strong affirmation of gender and sexual diversity and the diversity of bodies, works out the meaning of consent to sexual activity, and, finally, reaches the argument's climax about pleasure.

Through these five hallmarks, the Manisexto offers a clarion call to live out the gendered and sexual aspects of identity and relationship with authenticity, compassion, and joy.

So, welcome to the revolution! A fresh, twenty-first-century script about gender. An emerging consensus on diversity. A consent-based approach to sexual well-being. A new vision of love.

Turn the page and join in the conversation. We'll start with the first and most fundamental commitment: to good sex.

Manisexto #1

POSITIVE SEXUALITY

Sexuality Is a Normal, Healthy, and Pleasurable Aspect of Being Human

Chapter 1

sex

It's Complicated

At the core of the cultural change we're charting lies the hot-button topic of sex—hot button, especially in America, for a couple of reasons.

The first reason is a universal one: human sexuality is complicated. Desire is complicated. Sexuality is perhaps the messiest aspect of human embodiment. It's about a lot, and the stakes can be high. It's what gets us naked and exposed. Sexuality represents our physicality as embodied selves, with all the potential that poses for ecstasy, intimacy, and reproduction but also assault, disease, and death. It represents a poignant crux of pleasure and danger, especially for women with their greater susceptibility to rape and their biology as child-bearers. Sex can be a pathway to knowledge of self, with dueling possibilities for insight and self-deception. At the core, it represents the human longing for connection in a world where love is fraught with risk.

> "Part of what's so exciting about sex, particularly with a new partner, is that it's an inherently alarming thing to do."

Here's a notion: *sex may be the riskiest thing we do to ourselves.* As we screw around, sex can screw us up. Certainly, sex can make your day—your night—but also break your heart, your bank account, your health. Sex

15

Even the definition is complicated. The terms *sex* and *sexuality* are used in various ways that cover a lot of territory. Are we talking coitus or chromosomes? Sex can be about gender identity: whether one identifies as male, female, or nonbinary. Sex can be about desire: how we are attracted to others. Sex can be about practice: intimate activities we engage in. Sex and sexuality have dimensions that include the biological (the physical body, genetics, hormones), the psychological (emotional and intellectual processes), the interpersonal (relationships, friends, family), and the sociocultural (the larger context in which we live; history, media, government). See, for example, the sex education website Scarleteen for a good discussion that shows the complexity of the term.

involves the vulnerability of opening heart and body to another. Reproduction, relationship, and emotional intimacy can all entail lifelong repercussions.

In another layer of complication, although sex is deeply personal and individualistic, it impacts the public sphere, making the stakes high at a societal level as well. The culture tries to tame and order this chaos, this disruptive/creative power of sexuality. Social institutions, such as governments, organized religion, and the media, all try to gain power by exerting a regulatory function over sexuality. They control what is considered legal versus illegal sex, sinful versus moral sex, mainstream versus marginalized sex.

Through such means, the culture mandates how we should live out our sexual lives, but there's a problem: sexual diversity has always been much wider than society has allowed. Moreover, the mandates about sex and gender roles have always been unbalanced, tipped toward the pleasure and power of those in positions of privilege. To give one example we'll examine in a later chapter, American artist Sophia Wallace makes the claim in her *Cliteracy* art installation that "freedom in society can be measured by the distribution of orgasms." From this provocative perspective, sex is about no less than human rights, citizenship, and democracy itself.

The second reason for the hot-button status of sex is more specific to America. America, of course, is a complicated entity itself. The United States is a big country, both in terms of the size of its population and its geographic spread. Its demographics and culture are marked by huge diversity. Its politics spans a

Marlene Dietrich.

Check out *Pleasure and Danger: Exploring Female Sexuality,* edited by Carole S. Vance, a collection of influential essays published in 1984 and discussed ever since for its framework of the duality of sex as both pleasurable and risky.

spectrum from far-right conservatives to far-left progressives, with radicals at both ends and a big messy middle. There is no one America. Nevertheless, scholars trace how the United States has a particularly troubled relationship with sexuality, marked by contradictory and often hypocritical attitudes rooted deep in the nation's history.

On the one hand, we bear the legacy of the Puritans wherein sexual behavior is strictly controlled. Any expression of sexuality outside tightly drawn moral boundaries remains suspect, if not deemed downright sinful. On the other hand is America's free love tradition dating back to the nineteenth century, linked to social utopian movements of that period, and connecting sexuality with pleasure and the freedom of personal choice.

"Sex: In America an obsession. In other parts of the world a fact." —Marlene Dietrich

So, yeah, hot button. Ambivalent, messy, high stakes. Fraught with double standards and mixed messages in the stories the culture feeds us:

Sex is good, yet sex is bad.
Sex is pleasurable, yet sex is dangerous.
You're a slut (or man-whore if you're a guy, which is actually sort of okay) if you do; you're a prude if you don't.

"When we're young, we begin to feel this pressure to have sex, but we are never really taught how to have sex safely, respectfully, and pleasurably. Our society has such a contradictory view on sex."

Overall, the erotic poses a puzzle: How to live out sexuality for the good. How best to experience and share its potential for pleasure and human connection, in either a one-time relationship or a lifetime commitment. Say you're on a dating app and the option opens up for casual hookup sex. How do you decide whether to do it or not? If you're having sex, how are you supposed to negotiate consent and ensure your pleasure? How do you keep yourself safe, and why are sexual violence and harassment still so maddeningly pervasive?

Or, what if *Fifty Shades* inspired you and the kinky play of BDSM and flavors outside the vanilla appeal: how do you ask for what you want without exposing yourself to the censure of a startled partner or the judgment of society calling you a perv? What if you have no desire and delight in your asexuality, but the culture insists you have to be partnered? What if you've discovered you really like a variety of partners and "one true love" just isn't your idea of happily ever after? Or, what if you and your one-true-love partner still happily lust for each other after a lifetime of marriage, but you feel aged-shamed by the culture as too over-the-hill for sex?

The conundrums of sexuality get portrayed in endless permutations arising from the pop culture wells of TV, film, fiction, social media, advertising, music, and more. From song lyrics to porn to *The Bachelor* to celebrity Instagram feeds, we consume imagery and stories about sex and love in massive quantity. Through these collective fantasy spaces of the popular culture, we explore over and over again how to make the erotic work out.

The present-day moment of gender and sexual revolution is getting American society to a cultural tipping point where its conflicted attitudes around sex have a chance to be resolved.

Finally, we're getting closer to good sex.

Chapter 2

WHAT DO WE MEAN BY "GOOD" SEX?

Good is the oldest, most general, and most commonly used term of commendation in the English language. Its roots twist back as far as the ninth century, into the earliest recorded stages of Old English and its Germanic language origins. It's a grand word, laden over time with rich connotations. So how does the term help articulate what we mean when we talk about "good sex" as the Manisexto's most fundamental commitment?

Let's start with the dual meanings the word carries of both *ethical* and *pleasurable*. I titled this book *Good Sex* very deliberately, in order to highlight how these two definitions intertwine. Good sex is sex that is good, as in ethical or morally commendable, and good, as in pleasurable. As to the ethical: good sex is consensual, does no harm, and impacts people's lives in positive ways. As to the pleasurable: good sex is hot! Erotic, sexy, stimulating, sensual. It satisfies desire and leads to physical and emotional enjoyment for all partners involved,

> *Good,* as defined by *Oxford English Dictionary*: "conforming to a high standard of morality or virtue; warranting moral approval, morally commendable; virtuous" and also "pleasing, appealing, or satisfying to the senses."

orgasms all around. In both senses, sex should *do* good and *feel* good. In both senses, sex *is* good.

This intertwining of the ethical and the pleasurable reflects an ancient and enduring belief that the good life, the life worth living, is a moral one that brings satisfaction to the person living that life. To do good feels good. The philosophical conviction in play here is that real happiness—a deep and mature happiness—comes from the sure self-knowledge that one is acting honorably. Knowing that one's conscience is clear produces contentment and a sense of ease.

Aristotle.

"Happiness depends upon ourselves." —Aristotle

Aristotle, a fourth-century BCE philosopher, developed this argument in classical Greece through the concept of *eudaimonia*, commonly translated as *happiness*. The term derives from the Greek word for "good," *eu*, joined to the word *daimon*, meaning "spirit," as in a guardian spirit or minor deity. The etymology suggests the blessedness of being protected by a benevolent god or of being like a god. Eudaimonia, as Aristotle explains in his *Nicomachean Ethics*, means doing well and living well. It represents the ancient Greek ideal of the virtuous life worth living.

This concept of personal well-being distinguishes eudaimonia from a different type of happiness: *hedonia*, translated as *delight*, *bliss*, or *pleasure*. This is the root of the English word *hedonism*, defined as the pursuit of pleasure and sensual self-indulgence. Eudaimonia and hedonia represent two distinct visions of what makes a person happy. According to Aristotle, a person who is living a good life values the deeper and lasting happiness of eudaimonia—not merely the shallow, fleeting pleasures of the moment of hedonism.

The delineation of these two varieties of happiness builds up the meaning of good sex. There's nothing wrong with the pursuit of sexual pleasure

Mae West.

as hedonism, as gratification of desire, as long as such pursuit of "good sex" doesn't violate "good sex"—as long as self-satisfaction doesn't come (so to speak) at the expense of others. The pursuit of pleasure is not unethical, in and of itself. What is unethical is a hedonistic pursuit of self-satisfaction that ignores the needs and wants of others—and that ignores the need of one's own self to live a deeper life of self-realization. To put it another way, sensual body pleasure (hedonism) is best enjoyed as one aspect of living a good and worthy life (eudaimonia). In both these senses of happiness, sex is meant for the good.

> ## "Good sex is like good bridge. If you don't have a good partner, you'd better have a good hand." —Mae West

Another word association is important here. *Good*, as linked in these enduring ways to ethics, pleasure, and happiness, also carries connotations of the divine. This sense is conveyed in the word history that intertwines *good* with the similar word *God*. Old English and later usage associate these two words and sometimes substitute *good* for *God*: the good is linked to the godly. It's the same link as the etymology of eudaimonia that ties happiness to the blessings of the gods.

This cluster of associations of the good with happiness and the divine continued into the very founding of American democracy. The preamble of the Declaration of Independence from 1776 states, "We hold these truths to be self-evident, that all men [feel free to read 'people'] are created equal, that they are endowed by their Creator with certain unalienable Rights, that among these are Life, Liberty, and the pursuit of Happiness." The United States is a nation founded upon the idea that humans have the right—a right viewed as God-given or divinely ordained—to pursue happiness. We believe it to be a true and good thing that people are meant to be happy. In the context of the Manisexto, we have the right to be happy in our gender identities and our sex lives, as long as we don't infringe on the rights and autonomy of others.

> "Because sex is so influential to your emotions, understanding your sexuality is a key process in becoming an overall happy person, but people seem to only kind of get that. Casual and premarital sex are way less stigmatized now, yet people still have these lingering beliefs that enjoying sex is immoral."

Whatever one's religious beliefs—whether or not one believes in some form of personal creator god or spiritual realm—a powerful intuition is at work in the association of the good and the godly. This insight adds depth to our understanding of human sexuality: when sex is good, there can be something transcendent to it. The spiritual aspect of sexuality has the potential to lift people out of the everyday, to alter regular states of consciousness, to offer respite and rapture through the thrill of living in our bodies in the now. Sexuality can take us beyond self to connect to others in some of life's deepest experiences of love and bonding.

> "Sex connects us to the soul of the world; it connects us to the soul of all things. It should be considered a sacred act."

Some religious traditions make the point explicit. The monotheistic religions—Judaism, Christianity, Islam—often viewed sexuality with suspicion because of its ability to derail reason and morality but nevertheless understood sex as an intrinsic part of the goodness of creation. For example, Augustine, an influential fourth- and fifth-century Church Father, framed the problem not as one of sexuality itself but of *concupiscence*: the inordinance of sexual desire; the involuntary, immoderate, and

Saint Augustine.

unruly nature of lust; the difficulty of keeping desire's excess in check through rationality and the will.

In biblical language, sexuality is central to God's plan for humanity, as reflected in the story of the creation of humans in Genesis, the first book of the Hebrew Bible and the Christian Old Testament: "God blessed them, saying: 'Be fertile and multiply, fill the earth'" (Gen. 1:28). In this story, sexuality is a command from God. The pleasure of sexuality is ordained as a gift from God. Sex is meant to be enjoyed by couples, to create the bonds not only of parenthood and family but also of intimate companionship. Sex is part of the sensual delight of embodiment that gives sweetness to relationship and life. "This, at last," says Adam about Eve, "is bone of my bones and flesh of my flesh!" (Gen. 2:23).

"Oh Lord, grant me chastity, but do not grant it yet." —Saint Augustine, *Confessions*

Making the point even more explicit is the view of sexuality as a sacred pathway of religious insight and knowledge. Within the long and complex history of esoteric or mystical traditions in the biblical religions, in Hindu and Buddhist tantra, and right up to modern-day New Age spirituality, sexual union represents divine union—whether understood as metaphor or as part of religious practice. Sexuality models the correspondence between a person's inner world and ultimate reality. Just as shared sexual passion binds soul mates together, so does the soul of the faithful unite with the beloved God, so do complementary aspects of the divine cohere into a whole, so is the tribe of Israel covenanted to their jealous god Yahweh, so is the Christian church bound to her bridegroom Christ. "Let him kiss me with the kisses of his mouth," says the biblical Song of Solomon, a central text in the wisdom literature of this tradition, "for your love is more delightful than wine" (Song of Sol. 1:2). Sexual ecstasy serves as a model

The Ecstasy of Saint Teresa (1647–52) by Bernini, in the Church of Santa Maria della Vittoria, Rome.

for spiritual ecstasy. Orgasm, as an intense shattering release, models the believer's release from the narrow (illusory, sinful) ego-self into the intensity of spiritual insight or enlightenment.

Precisely what Augustine saw as negative—the very inordinance of sexuality, its mode of powerful and destabilizing excess—can be a dazzling and divine positive. The erotic, after all, is named after a god: in ancient Greek religion, Eros is one of the original primordial gods who brings the cosmos into being. The turbulence of sexual desire opens up energy and the power of elemental creativity. It is this generative aspect of sexuality that accounts for its core association with the divine.

The emphasis on generativity leads to the final step in a delineation of good sex: sex is about the literal creation of new life. Sexuality is a good, "a thing that is beneficial," to cite yet another definition of the word *good*: that which has advantage, sense, use, utility, point. From a human biological standpoint, a central purpose of sexual activity is reproduction. In this sense, sex is not just a good thing but is also necessary for the continuation of the species. Sexual reproduction creates the grand sweep of history and time: our past and our wider selves through genetic links to ancestors and extended family, and the hope of the future through generations to come.

Here, the goodness of sexuality extends into the family and impacts people's lives in ways that include parenthood. It's an obvious statement but one that bears making from the outset: we are all here because of the union of an egg and a sperm. There are no babies, no families, no furtherance of humanity, without sexuality. Even taking into account the advent of medically assisted reproductive technologies to treat infertility and to create more options for single people and same-sex couples to become parents, sexual intercourse remains the standard pathway to pregnancy and childbirth.

I am not saying that sex has to be reproductive for it to be good. Nonreproductive sexual acts are no less good or less natural than acts of reproductive sex. It's far too simple to say that the point of sex is to make babies. People engage in sexual acts for lots of good reasons, seeking out a variety of different goods— pleasure, fun, excitement, intimacy, con-

One possible outcome of good sex!

nection, stress release, maybe even a demonstration of prowess or a way to burn calories. There is danger in "repro-centrism," the insistence that parenthood is our destiny and that a person's life is not complete without children. Such an insistence is coercive. It's captured in sayings like "The day my child was born was the happiest day of my life" (for me, it felt like the day I was run over by a truck) and "Children are a blessing from God." These statements are certainly true for some people, but they can also feel overblown and do a lot of harm. Repro-centrism targets women in particular. The notion that a woman should become a mother—that motherhood is the essence of a good woman and her highest calling—still holds too much cultural sway. As does the suspicion that there's something wrong with a gal who simply doesn't want to raise kids.

> "The female organ is not just a device that exists for men to push into and babies to push out of."

Again, don't mistake me, parenthood *can* be a wonderful experience. The parent-child bond can be one of life's most meaningful and fulfilling relationships. And for a woman to conceive, gestate, birth, and perhaps breastfeed a child can be a literally awesome experience—an awe-filled experience of her body as a creative life force, with the very power of a Mother Nature earth goddess to bring forth new being. But there's no reason why this vision of life must be one-size-fits-all.

My mom, a very good mother, once told me she thinks there is something selfish about not wanting to have children. Someone, presumably, must continue the human species, and it's hard work. For her, choosing to be childless felt like copping out, not doing your part, focusing too much on yourself, and, in the process, missing out on something precious. Yet not everyone needs to be a parent, and not everyone is cut out to be the good parent that every child deserves. A person can absolutely be a fulfilled, mature, happy adult without children. There are plenty of other ways to live a creative and generative life, plenty of ways to experience family bonds and to contribute to community and society.

The ability of sex to create new life is one source of its power—but also its anxiety, if getting pregnant isn't what you want. Ideally, people have a choice about when and whether they have kids. Ideally, pregnancy is planned and desired. Ideally, babies are born to loving adults who have the inclination, time, and resources to be good parents. And ideally, society supports families. The new gender and sexual revolution embraces "strong family values," a term that rises far above partisan political divides and offers meaningful advocacy to families of all sorts. Here, key components of good sex include comprehensive sex education; the ready availability of birth control and family planning choices; high-quality reproductive health care, prenatal care, and woman-centered birthing options, including doulas and midwives; accessible and excellent childcare options; and a wide range of family-centered policies in schools, the government, and the workplace.

The goodness of sex is good in all these ways. Good sex is ethical, pleasurable, happiness-inducing, creative, sometimes even transcendent, and strongly supportive of family.

Overall, this vision is what's called *sex-positivity*. But *sex-positive* is a term easily misunderstood—and one hard to make real.

Time to dig a little deeper.

Chapter 3

THE MISUNDERSTOOD MEANING OF "SEX-POSITIVE"

To refer in these various ways to good sex—to say that sex is meant to be a good thing—is to say, on the one hand, that sexuality is a normal, healthy, and pleasurable aspect of being human and, on the other hand, that people have the right to their sexual choices, as long as those choices are consensual and uphold partners' best interests and autonomy. To say all this is to be *sex-positive* or committed to *positive sexuality*.

To be sex-positive is to have a positive attitude—an open-minded, tolerant, accepting attitude—toward sexuality. Sex educator Dr. Emily Nagoski describes it succinctly: "Shame-free, healthy, good for you, beneficial. Sex-positivity, it turns out, says, 'Sex? It's positive!'" A popular saying that captures the essence of this approach: "Don't yuk someone else's yum." Passion comes in many flavors. Some people love chocolate ice cream; others lust after strawberry (don't even get me started on pistachio gelato). But we don't wage ice cream wars or condemn people to hell for their frozen dessert choices. Sexual orientation and desire run a broad gamut from the straight-up vanilla to the rainbow with sprinkles. Not everyone wants the same things or is turned on by the same practices in the bedroom. As

> #sexpositive: **Sex-positivity** is the belief (1) that sexuality is a normal, healthy, and pleasurable aspect of being human and (2) that people have the right to all sexual choices that are consensual and uphold partners' best interests and autonomy.

long as partners are adults who are consenting in meaningful ways—well, then, you might not like something for yourself, but you don't have to condemn it for everyone else. The sex-positive conviction is that people should not be shamed, discriminated against, or criminalized for their consensual sexual choices.

The move of this sex-positive ethic onto Main Street signals a historic cultural shift. If you were around when *Fifty Shades of Grey* came out in 2011, you'll remember how it seemed everyone bought a copy or snuck a peek. E. L. James's erotic romance set records as the fastest-selling paperback of all time and went on to become the top-selling novel of the decade. Eva Illouz, an international scholar on emotions and communication, sees evidence in the *Fifty Shades* trilogy's stratospheric success of an "immense change in values that must have occurred in Western culture—as dramatic a change, one might say, as electricity and indoor plumbing." We can debate whether the *Fifty Shades* phenomenon was truly sex-positive, but the very fact of the trilogy's massive popularity speaks to how contemporary society has become more open about sexuality.

In another example, acceptance of same-sex marriage continues to grow yearly, from rates of 27 percent in 1996 to 63 percent of American adults supporting same-sex marriage in 2019. Even more telling? This increase is largely due to generational change. The highest acceptance rates—a whopping 83 percent—are among young Americans aged eighteen to twenty-nine, so there's every reason to expect support to grow even more over time.

> "Sex is PERSONAL.
> Sex is something different for everyone."

This move toward more sex-positive attitudes and public policies has become one of the most significant cultural trends to work its way into the recent mainstream. But the concept of positive sexuality is, as I said, an easy one to misunderstand. If *sex-positive* conjures in your mind visions of a license for wild DTF (down to fuck) orgies in the street, that's the misunderstanding right there. It gets the notion of sex-positivity wrong, in two problematic ways.

First, while sex-positivity entails a more open and tolerant attitude toward sexuality, it absolutely does not mean anything goes. It's a false assumption that a commitment to diversity and inclusion gives people carte blanche to indulge in any and all sexual desires, no matter the consequences. The irony is, sex-positivity actually has a very strong moral code. It imposes an ethical framework through its uncompromising commitment to full and informed consent: the condition that sexual activity be adult, free of coercion, safe, and mutually desirable.

> "I believe everyone should be able to explore their sexual interest so long as no one is getting hurt in the process."

We'll talk a lot more in chapter 4 about the meaning of consent. For now, it's important to note that sex-positivity is not all about sexy fun and games. It's about exercising freedom in responsible ways. It's about being sensitive to problems of sexual injustice and gender inequity in society. It's about healthy decision-making and good communication, about respect for oneself and one's partners. Positive sexuality always entails *ethical* sex.

Here's the second misunderstanding to clear up from the get-go. Sex-positivity does not mean you need to be having lots of hot sex all the time or you're a loser who's missing out. The culture requires sex but the Manisexto doesn't. Again, perhaps ironically, there is no requirement within sex-positivity for anyone to be more sexually active or for sexuality to occupy more space in the

GGG: A nice bit of sex-positive urban lingo. GGG stands for good, giving, and game. Sex advice columnist and podcaster Dan Savage, author of *Savage Love*, coined the term to evaluate what makes for a good sexual partner. As Savage explains it: "Think 'good in bed,' 'giving equal time and equal pleasure' and 'game for anything—within reason.'"

culture. The story of sex as told in America has often been prescriptive, telling people about the sex life they need to have, but in ways that can do more harm than good. The romance narrative, for example, orders us to *Find your one true love and live happily ever after*, in its endless stream of Hollywood rom-coms and Harlequin romance novels. Meanwhile, *Live life hot and sexy*, the porn culture pants in our ear. And the advertising industry, happy to take our money, insists on its consumer messages: *Style yourself as a manly stud or a feminine sex goddess*.

All this advice adds up to a whole lot of crazy-making pressure. Pressure to want sex, to have sex, to look sexy, so as not to fail at what the culture deems so vitally important. But sometimes the best sex is no sex. And the best question is what sex is worth having, with whom and when. The new gender and sexual revolution encourages people to make thoughtful choices for themselves, choices that are consistent with their personal values and consensual desires, including the very fine choice to say "No" or "Not now."

> "Sexuality is something that should be treated and felt as liberating and that should be not only accepted but celebrated today."

Another way to clarify the meaning of sex-positivity is to think about its opposite, sex-negativity. The sex-negative, as the opposite of the sex-positive, consists of actions and attitudes that negate the goodness of sexuality, that pair sexuality with violence, oppression, coercion, fear, guilt, anxiety, stigma, and shame. Nonconsensual sex—all forms of sexual abuse, harassment, exploitation, and assault, including human trafficking—epitomizes sex-negativity at its very worst. Rape is a perversion of sexuality precisely because it turns sex into power over another person, as opposed to shared "power with" (more on that contrast in chapter 18). Sexually abusive people weaponize sex as a means to exert exploitative dominance over others, often over vulnerable and marginalized people who have less power and protection in society. The women's movement and feminism have been instrumental in analysis and advocacy around such trauma.

It's hard to be sex-positive if you feel surrounded by, or victimized by, ongoing sex-negative attitudes and practices. Despite the rising trend of positive sexuality in society, the enduring aspects of sex-negativity act as a brake against continued progress. In a culture where rape remains all too common and rapists often go unpunished, to tell a survivor they should be more sex-positive simply perpetrates another form of assault. In a homophobic society, telling a closeted gay or lesbian person to be out and sex-positive misses the point as well: they often *can't*, for risk of harm to themselves. From this perspective, being able to hold a sex-positive viewpoint and express it openly is a privilege in itself.

The new gender and sexual revolution is working to actualize sex-positivity more fully, but the movement is far from complete. Closer than ever before; not there yet. Through the Manisexto's vision of sexual justice, gender equity, and the normalization of diversity, we have it within our grasp to realize much more fully a future of good sex.

> "Changing the conversation to be more sex-positive and less about just abstinence and pregnancy will encourage everyone to speak up about the things they feel or that they are unsure of. It would help establish a higher level of respect for sexual partners as well as respect for yourself."

What remains standing in the way?

Partly, it's the story of sex in America, a story so fraught and ambivalent that it allows the misunderstandings we've traced to take hold. It makes uprooting them difficult.

To proceed further, we have to go back to that troubled American relationship with sexuality that we discussed earlier and clear some of the roadblocks out of the way.

Chapter 4

THE TWO-SIDED STORY OF SEX IN AMERICA

America as "puritanical." We hear this often, but what does it mean?

The term harkens back to a group of the country's earliest European immigrants—the Puritans—who established the Massachusetts Bay Colony in the seventeenth century. They fled England, seeking freedom to practice their particular form of Christianity. As a loose political and theological movement, their name derives from members' desire to purify the Church of England as well as their emphasis on moral purity. *Puritanical*, as a pejorative term, now conjures visions of austere religion, a censorious attitude, and strict demands for adherence to behavioral rules.

The heritage of the Puritans lives on in the United States they helped found through an enduring leeriness toward sex. We see the persistence of this puritan impulse in what's sometimes referred to as "pearl clutching": a shocked, wide-eyed, disapproving stance of *Oh, my! Do people really do that?* and *That must stop at once!* (Cue visual of an older lady, hand to throat, catching hold of her proverbial string of pearls, but note also the misogyny of that stereotype, as if only women are stodgy reactionaries.)

Where do these narratives about sexuality come from? How does a society use them to regulate its people's attitudes and behaviors? The high-stakes nature of sexuality certainly poses a challenge for any society. To

> "Life in Lubbock, Texas, taught me two things. One is that God loves you and you're going to burn in hell. The other is that sex is the most awful, dirty thing on the face of the earth and you should save it for someone you love." —Butch Hancock, singer/songwriter

better understand America's particular story about sex, we can turn to the work of sociologists John H. Gagnon and William Simon. They developed an influential theory about how societies navigate this challenge by crafting stories or "scripts" about sexuality.

According to Gagnon and Simon, these sexual scripts train people in what counts as proper conduct or allowable sexual behavior in any given time and place. The culture tells us how to live out our sexuality, but people also craft their own stories that either fall in line with the dominant discourse or tell a counternarrative. Sexual scripts interact with gender scripts—stories about what it means to be a man or a woman, cultural codes that teach you how to perform your gender role "properly," in accordance with the dominant norms—that, again, people either enact or push back against, par-

> Gagnon and Simon described sexual scripts as functioning at three levels: the level of the *cultural* script (society-wide narratives that provide the framework and convey the standard ideology and expectations around sex), the *interpersonal* script (scenarios linked to social interaction between people), and the *intrapsychic* script (private fantasies and conditioned triggers of desire).

ticularly when the role doesn't make for a good fit. Social script theory thus argues that norms about sexuality and gender are not purely natural or God-given but are shaped by societal expectation and interaction. The script gains its authority, however, precisely through the claim that these norms are *not* a product of the culture but a fact of the natural order or divine will.

What is the sexual script in American culture? It's actually twofold—and contradictory. That's why the culture often feels puritanical and porn-saturated, both at the same time: a nation shaped by a Puritan founding history, inhabiting a pop culture landscape saturated with sex. America talks about sex through two contrasting scripts that function as the legacy of two warring impulses, two different master narratives twisted together in the country's history. The root of this complicated American attitude toward sex is the *puritan* versus the *free love* view of sexuality and sin, a dynamic itself rooted deep in Christian theology.

While the American reserve and squeamishness about sex speak to the influence of the early Puritans, it's not entirely fair that we use their name to mean prudish and anti-sex. The history and theology are more complex than this derogatory stereotype suggests. Like Augustine, Puritans were not against sex, per se. They saw sex in marriage as good.

> Some people still base their rejection of same-sex romance on the argument that such relationships aren't natural or part of God's plan—**God didn't create them Adam and Steve**—but script theory demonstrates how social factors normalize heterosexuality, link it to male-led gender roles, turn it into the only show in town, and dress it up in white-wedding, pretty-princess romance ideology.

Women were entitled to sex from their husbands, partly so they could have children; a husband's impotence was an allowable reason for a woman to request divorce. Even more so, sexual pleasure in marriage was held to be good and fitting and sanctioned by God. Puritans could be quite sex-positive, delighting in the lusty bed play of husband and wife.

It's sex *outside* these sanctioned limits that poses a problem. Here's where this particular sexual script starts to sound rather, well, *puritanical*. The script mandates that sex must be married, heterosexual, monogamous, reproductive, not too kinky, and patriarchal—part

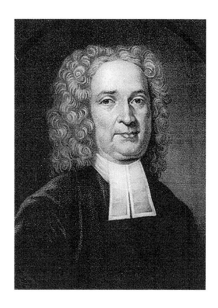

John Cotton, a revered Puritan minister of the Massachusetts Bay Colony, preached a 1694 wedding sermon on the goodness of marriage and sex using the biblical phrase that woman is "companion and helpmeet" to man (Gen. 2:18). "She is a most sweet and intimate companion, and an entire friend; there is no stricter or sweeter friendship than conjugal; as it was the first in the world, so it is most natural."

Scene from Nathaniel Hawthorne's classic American novel *The Scarlet Letter*.

of a male-led structure of family and society. Yes, sex is good—even very good—but the goodness adheres only within these strict limits said to define moral purity. Violating the norms comes at a high price. This is true especially for women: the scarlet letter A for *adulterer* continues in double-standard purity codes that still function to regulate the sexual behavior of women, more so than men, and that punish deviation from the norm.

Today, women get branded with a scarlet S: *she's such a slut*. The sneer echoes across college campuses in the ritual of the morning-after-the-night-before "walk of shame," she in her heels, tugging on her skirt too short for the morning sunlight, the guy getting high fives back at the frat house. This puritan version of America's sexual script—the story that the culture tells its people about sex—blends elements of traditional gender roles, religion, and capitalism (sex as reproductive, making new workers for farm and factory and citizens for the state). The script, with its regulatory mechanism of slut-shaming, benefits the status quo and keeps intact entrenched systems of male power and control.

> "A feeling of deep shame regarding sex was instilled in me by the Southern Baptist church of my youth. I remember being required to purchase one-piece swimsuits for a church retreat, as our two-pieces would 'tempt the boys.' So much weight was placed on sex as a sacred but forbidden act. These notions led me to develop severe anxiety regarding sex that I still struggle with today. I cried every single time I left the house of my freshman-year boyfriend, wracked with such intense feelings of guilt and fear that I would be eternally damned. Even following my departure from faith, I struggle with panic attacks with every new partner."

In contrast to the puritan sexual script is the script of America's free love movement of sexual liberation. The free love script stands in the two-thousand-year-old history of what scholars call *antinomianism* in Christian thought. *Nomos* means "law" in classical Greek; *antinomian* refers to the "anti-law" tradition in Christianity. An early instance of antinomian free love provokes the apostle Paul to write to the Corinthians in his New

John Humphrey Noyes, founder of the Oneida Community, viewed "conventional marriage both as a form of legalism from which Christians should be free and as a selfish institution in which men exerted rights of ownership over women." —The Oneida Community Collection, Syracuse University Library

Testament letter. The first-century CE community of Christian converts in Corinth, Greece, had apparently been indulging in sexual licentiousness—Paul mentions a "man living with his father's wife" (1 Cor. 5:1), adultery, prostitution (1 Cor. 6:9)—with the belief that faith in Christ frees them from the old law and the sexual purity codes of the Hebrew Bible. Paul counters this anti-law argument: "All is permitted, although not all is edifying" (1 Cor. 10:23). Paul's corrective points out a misunderstanding: being freed from some laws doesn't mean you're freed from all laws.

But what laws, then, *are* binding, and how are we to know? Antinomians raise questions about the efficacy of the law or whatever a society takes to be the standard moral order. They view society's traditional moral rules as nonbinding and consider at least some norms of religion or society as open to revision based on new insight. Versions of the antinomian controversy raged throughout Christian history, debated by theologians and enacted by various groups. Early Christianity and Paul himself are antinomian in their rejection of many Jewish laws, as the new sect of the Christ-followers separated itself from its origins in Judaism. Paul, for example, rejects the Jewish laws of circumcision and kosher dietary practice. Centuries later, the Protestant Reformation would be antinomian in its rejection of Catholic Church law on various points such as the celibacy of the clergy.

The question animating these debates is how correct any particular set of behavioral rules is in aiding the individual and the community to achieve the good. And who gets to decide? Is the authority for setting and revising the rules to be individual conscience, societal tradition, new consensus, government regulation, religious claims about God's will, or something else entirely?

In terms of sexuality—who is allowed to marry or be sexually intimate with whom, what makes sex "good" in our dual sense of ethical and pleasurable—the antinomian debate evolved in America into what became known as the free love movement. From the nineteenth century to the 1960s to today, this version of America's story about sex argues for *freedom from* the received sexual norms and *freedom to* rewrite these sexual scripts. The free love movement was complex, with different aims, and often used "free" in different senses: that people should be free to choose the love partner they please, that unions should be free from the interference of governmental marriage and divorce laws, that parenthood should be voluntary through freely available birth control (often outlawed by US and state governments well into the twentieth century).

> "Sex is not a secret we all must bear but rather is a shared, lived experience that we often minimize in America for the sake of puritanical social norms and expectations."

Some, but not all, free love thinkers advocated against monogamy as a restriction of individual freedom. Many explicitly linked free love to the early women's rights movement, comparing marriage to slavery in a time when the law granted men control over a wife's money and property and allowed a husband to beat and rape a wife. Antinomian reform efforts led to experimental social utopian communities such as Oneida, in the state of New York, founded in 1848 by the Christian writer John Humphrey Noyes. Noyes is the one who coined the term *free love*, as well as *complex marriage*, to describe the open, although still regulated, sexual relationships practiced by the members of the Oneida community.

A century later, the sexual liberation movement of the 1960s echoed many of these same principles raised by various nineteenth-century free love advocates: sex outside traditional marriage, birth control, women's rights. New elements entered the debate as well. Gay rights

Victoria Woodhull established the first female stockbrokerage on Wall Street and, in 1872, became the first woman to run for US president. She declared, "Yes, I am a Free Lover. I have an inalienable, constitutional and natural right to love whom I may."

As part of the sexual liberation movement of the 1960s, "Make love not war" became the rallying cry of the day.

marched onto the scene—now celebrated in annual Pride parades—after a 1969 police raid on a New York City gay bar resulted in the watershed Stonewall uprisings (notably led by transgender women of color). Protests against censorship followed landmark obscenity trials for the long-banned novel *Lady Chatterley's Lover*. Anti-war activism swelled as countercultural protesters linked personal freedom to political freedom: "Make love not war" became the rallying cry of the day.

This twentieth-century antinomian version of the sexual script aligned with a long-standing American defense of individual rights, personal autonomy, and self-determination. It aligned with libertarian concerns about government overreach—that government had no place in the privacy of the nation's bedrooms. It resonated with America's overall championing of freedom as a central ideal, although never yet a full reality achieved equitably for all.

This freedom refrain—to unchain sexuality from unnecessary restrictions, to liberate love from restraints that impede the good that sexuality makes possible—resounds from biblical Corinth, to Renaissance Germany, to nineteenth-century Oneida, to 1967 San Francisco when one hundred thousand hippies gathered for the "Summer of Love," to the American college hookup scene.

Which brings us to the present.

Chapter 5

ROMANCING THE PURITAN

The two-sided story of sex in America follows the broad historical sweep of the puritan versus the antinomian sexual scripts. The problem, however, is that neither script is ultimately satisfactory or workable as a basis for civic life. Think of them as pendulum swings on the question of what makes sex good. When the pendulum swings too far in the direction of the puritanical, we get an overemphasis on good as defined solely by the strict adherence to a narrow set of moral standards: an overemphasis on good-as-in-ethical. When the pendulum swings in the opposite direction, all the way toward antinomian free love, we get an overemphasis on good as defined by sex breaking free of those strict standards: an overemphasis on good-as-in-pleasurable.

On both sides of the pendulum swing, irony abounds. The irony of the puritan script is the larger irony of America's founding narrative: we are the land of the free, yet we insist that everybody must fit into a heterosexual box. We defend the primacy of individual rights, yet we prohibit and shame individual variation from the gender script (*boys don't cry*; *a lady doesn't raise her voice*), as if there were only one way to be a good man or good woman. The very notion of narrow and compulsory scripts for gender and sexuality violates the freedom and individuality so central to America, yet only recently has the pressure to conform eased up and the pearl-clutching protest started to die down.

"It is ironic that many Americans view the U.S. as the champion for human rights both domestically and internationally, yet we are not entitled to the right of comprehensive sex education. Americans are borderline obsessed with their rights: the right to own a gun, to not wear a mask, to do and say whatever they want because this is America and we're free! It is so frustrating to know I live in a 'developed' country that has been taught to us as 'the greatest country in the world,' then to grow up and learn how ignorant I am because the education system failed me and so many of my peers."

There's an irony on the other side of the pendulum, too: the free love movement has failed to result in a widespread culture of good sex. Free love, in its nineteenth- and twentieth-century forms, certainly had its successes. Birth control is now available and generally noncontroversial (although abortion is another debate). Family law more thoroughly enshrines principles of equality through same-sex marriage and more gender-neutral marriage, divorce, and child custody laws (although spousal violence continues to disadvantage women). But the problem is not simply that the sexual revolution remains incomplete. It's that the free love movement bogged down its own progress through persistent blind spots. It failed to embrace the full implications of inclusive feminism: not only gender equity but a deep acknowledgment of the intersection of systems of oppression. While it sought sexual liberation, it was slow to grasp how problems of sexual oppression intersected with and were made worse by problems of racism, ageism, ableism, classism, and more.

"I'm all for the sexual revolution and free love but we have to address sexual encounters as dynamic interactions. We need to address issues of power, of pleasure for all parties, respect, responsibility to protect physical and emotional health, and more."

The irony continues into the present day. Much of the college hookup scene, for example, is not sex-positive. What some bemoan as America's gone-to-hell-in-a-handbasket sexually permissive culture, I bemoan as well. Not because some young people are having no-strings-attached sex, but because so much of this sex, particularly for women, is bad sex. Too drunken to be fully consensual, with one-sided pleasure and an orgasm gap (more on that in chapter 20), and surrounded more by anxiety and peer pressure than mutual desire.

In the historical and philosophical back-and-forth of America's sexual script, the puritan impulse argues "Sex has to be *this* way" and insists on strict moral observance. The antinomian impulse argues "People should get to decide for themselves" and insists on the freedom of personal choice. Puritanism demands adherence to rules to which everyone must be subject. Free love demands to redefine the rules, in order to ensure equity and justice for everyone. Two profound truths compete. It is good to live within moral boundaries, as say the Puritans, and it is good to live free from unjust boundaries, as say the antinomians. Both convictions align with central American values: the equal rule of law, on the one hand; civil disobedience in defense of individual and minority rights, on the other hand. But both truths, both values, are vulnerable to exaggeration and to falling short of their own ideal.

Inclusive feminism and *intersectional feminism* refer to contemporary approaches to gender equity. Mainstream feminism initially focused on the experience of white middle- and upper-class women. Feminist analysis and activism today aims to be more inclusive, acknowledging the significant differences among the experiences and identities of women, particularly for women of color dealing with the oppression of racism. *Intersectionality* sees identity as shaped simultaneously by many categories that impact people's experience of privilege or of discrimination in society, such that feminism's traditional focus on categories of sex and gender is not complete unless it also includes categories of race and ethnicity, class or socioeconomic status, sexual orientation, age, religion, disability, and more.

The problem with the puritan impulse lies in its restrictiveness. Its ideal of ethical purity shines bright with moral outrage against wrongdoing, but puritanism betrays its idealism by insisting on too narrow an expression of the ideal. The narrowness hurts moral outliers, those people seeking to live a good life true to their authentic sense of self and to engage in consensual relationships. Their only sin is living outside the traditionally narrow boundaries of acceptable gender and sexual identity. Their only sin is diversity. Against them, moral outrage is misdirected.

> "In the US, a lot of our laws have to do with religion, like they might as well have copied and pasted the bible. Like, why was it even a thing to be able to FIRE SOMEONE because of their sexuality? The job still gets done. Period."

The problem with free love lies in its lack of limits. The problem stems from a failure to define clearly the principle acting as a brake against that slippery slope where anything goes. The fear is often exaggerated into a moral panic, but the concern about excessive openness is nonetheless legitimate. What maxim guides moral decision-making about where to draw the line once traditional rules are jettisoned? As the apostle Paul wrote, not all is edifying. We do need outrage against sexual wrongdoing. Freedom is not absolute, and not everything is okay.

Our present-day moment of gender and sexual revolution seeks to address the tension in play between these two impulses. It resolves the contradictory legacy of the American story of sex by drawing on resources from both the puritan and the antinomian sexual scripts and weaving these elements together. It aims for a story about transformed notions of gender roles and sex life amid the persistent question of which laws to reject and what new limits to impose. By defining good sex in terms of the ethical and the pleasurable, it offers a new positive story of sex in America.

From the puritan script, the Manisexto draws the fierce and uncompromising demand that sex must be ethical—morally pure, if you will. The new gender and sexual revolution has its own streak of puritanism, its own unbending moral backbone. Through the #MeToo movement, it calls for adherence to enforceable rules of behavior. It draws a hard line against sexual wrongdoing: *Across this line, sexual behavior is not ethical and will not be tolerated.* Sexual relationships must be consensual, occurring within the moral bounds of mutual agreement and respect. The revolution has its own scarlet letter: *R* for rapist. Today, more clearly than ever before, we condemn all forms of nonconsensual and manipulative sex: rape, abuse, harassment, exploitation, grooming, coercion. No more sweeping it under the rug.

From the script of free love, the Manisexto draws the frolicsome and unapologetic demand that sex be pleasurable, that people have a *right* to access sexual pleasure—not only heterosexuals and socially empowered men, but everyone operating within those moral bounds of mutual consent and respect. The new gender and sexual revolution champions a courageous quest for justice in the fight against oppression. It embraces a bold openness to the new. Precisely because entrenched sexual scripts have failed to support the equitable flourishing of all, we need to write more democratic scripts. The story of sex in America must support our most dearly held democratic values: equality, civil rights, individual choice. In short, sexual justice. Sexual scripts must treat everyone the same and accommodate the broadest diversity, through the protection of people who have been marginalized and unfairly stigmatized.

"Our society was founded by white men who wanted control over everything. We are finally at a point where people are no longer standing for the outdated, closed-minded norms, such as only a man and woman being legally married and also women's rights and racial injustice. The people who are fighting and protesting for justice today are the ones to reshape the generations to come. All it takes is one person to make a difference and spark awareness and change the system."

Here, if the puritan impulse called out free love on its moral laxity—the hippie's blissed-out *It's all good, dude* rings rather clueless—then free love calls out puritanism on its hypocrisy. The gender script has held women to the puritan ideal while allowing men greater leeway to experiment or stray, even if only in a wink-wink, boys-will-be-boys sort of way: *You can't keep a stallion in the stable.* No more hypocritical double standards. Today, it's high time for full equity and inclusion. High time to end slut-shaming, homophobia, and transphobia.

Sex-positivity defines good sex as ethical and pleasurable, both at the same time. This positive sexuality forms the foundation of the Manisexto and the basis for all that follows. The emerging new sexual script balances American historical antecedents of puritanism and free love into a fresh story about gender and sexuality, one that aims to maximize happiness and fulfillment.

But we're just getting started.

The next element, after this commitment to positive sexuality, is an equally fundamental commitment to diversity. The romantic matchup of a man and woman who embody standard gender norms remains a fine way to live a good life, but it's no longer the only game in town.

Manisexto #2

EQUITY AND INCLUSION

Gender and Sexual Identities Are Diverse—and That's Okay

Chapter 6

WHY DIVERSITY MATTERS ACROSS THE RAINBOW SPECTRUM, FOR US ALL

Today, people talk a lot more about diversity of gender and sexual identity than they did in the past. Used to be, the only options were a binary of female or male. Girl or boy, woman or man, tick the *F* box or the *M* box. And heterosexual wasn't an option; it was the assumed default for everyone.

This is not to deny the rich history of gay, lesbian, and transgender life. People have always found ways to live out their true selves with authenticity, within subcultures of resistance. If we fail to acknowledge this queer history of courage and resilience, we risk erasing people's lives in a damaging fiction of the past. So it's not that everyone was straight, but that society was highly *heteronormative*. A straight lifestyle was the only one that carried full legal and social sanctions. With the gay rights movement of the twentieth century, the broader diversity of gender and sexual identity began slowly to be accepted. The LGBT abbreviation spells out this diversity:

not just straight and male or female from birth, but *L* for lesbian, *G* for gay, *B* for bisexual, and *T* for transgender.

With the twenty-first century, the closet door swung open wider still. An even fuller alphabet of description came into play—LGBTQIA+—with more letters added as acknowledgment of diversity grew: *Q* for queer (an umbrella term adopted by sexual and gender minorities), *I* for intersex, *A* for asexual, and the plus sign to indicate an ongoing openness to other understandings of identity.

> "My high school didn't ***forbid*** same-sex couples from going to prom together, but you could tell the school didn't really like it. They only let you buy couples tickets if you were a guy and a girl. Same-sex couples had to buy singles tickets, which were more expensive."

#diversity: The National Education Association's *Diversity Toolkit* introduction: "Diversity can be defined as the sum of the ways that people are both alike and different. The dimensions of diversity include race, ethnicity, gender, sexual orientation, language, culture, religion, mental and physical ability, class, and immigration status. . . . Full acceptance of diversity is a major principle of social justice." Diversity of personal identity also includes aspects such as age, political ideology, education, family status, military experience, cognitive style, communication style, and more.

Gender is coming to be recognized not as a simple binary but as something more complex, with a range of fluid meanings and expressions beyond the traditional norms of male as "masculine" and female as "feminine." Although binary terms such as *girls/guys* and *women/men* present a convenient shorthand of language, newer terms such as *gender-nonconforming*, *nonbinary*, and *gender-queer* describe these expanded understandings. Some people use *they/them* as a singular pronoun, or alternative new pronouns, to claim a sense of self outside the gender binary. *Two-spirit* is sometimes added from the context of Native American or First Nations cultures as a third gender term for some-

The original rainbow flag, designed by activist Gilbert Baker, flew at the San Francisco Gay Freedom Day Parade in June 1978.

one who embodies both male and female spirits. Gender and sexuality become a spectrum—often symbolized by the rainbow stripes of the iconic Pride flag.

In America, any consideration of diversity must continue to reckon hard with the bull's-eye centrality of racial inequity in our country and its history. Increasingly, however, sexuality and gender have become key concerns in these equity and inclusion debates. We are in the midst of a sea change moving society in the direction of greater acceptance for gender and sexual diversity. Such change forms part of a centuries-long progression in American and world history toward fuller recognition of human rights: the end of legalized slavery, the en-

Heteronormative describes the presumption that everyone is heterosexual and that heterosexuality is the proper, normal, and appropriate way to express one's sexuality. To be heteronormative is to believe that romance and sex should only happen between a man and a woman. Societies support heteronormativity through institutions and expectations that privilege opposite-sex relationships and that stigmatize or discriminate against same-sex relationships. Examples can include marriage laws, representation in TV and film, and even a high school's policy on prom dates.

Intersex is an umbrella term for people born with one of about two dozen various conditions that result in differences of sex development. These conditions can involve the chromosomes, hormones, internal sex organs, or genitals, such that the body does not match the typical binary definition of male and female bodies. The United Nations promotes intersex awareness as part of "Free and Equal," its groundbreaking global campaign for equal rights and fair treatment of LGBTI people all around the world.

Along with the term *bisexual,* which refers to people who are sexually or romantically attracted to both women and men, an increasingly common term is *pansexual,* from the Greek prefix *pan-,* meaning "all" or "every." People who identify as pansexual are attracted to others without regard to a partner's gender or sexual identity. A nifty little description is that they are attracted to "hearts and not parts."

franchisement of women, the establishment of equal voting rights, the expansion of access for people with disabilities. Freedom grows. Increasingly, the rights of sexual and gender minority populations are protected through changes in law, health care, educational policy, media representation, employment practices, and the everyday attitudes of people in the general public.

"I am so grateful to be living in a time period where I don't feel endangered or outcast as a result of my identity, but I know not everyone is fortunate enough to have that experience."

American society is coming to *embrace* gender and sexual diversity like never before. Not absolutely, of course, and not across the board. Angry resistance and backlash exist. Not everyone who is different from the norm can be safely out. But among young people in particular, this expansion of the culture's permitted scripts is pervasive—even startling in the speed and scope of the cultural shift. As sociologist Barbara Risman notes, "This is the first time in history that young people are publically demanding to be identified without a gender at all, rejecting the 'gender binary' outright." Generation Z young adults aged eighteen to twenty-three are leading the way in rewriting these gender rules and the wider sexual scripts. A 2020 Gallup poll showed that one in six Gen Zers, or 15.9 percent, identity as LGBTQ—the highest rate ever among all age groups. It represents a massive generational shift. Among Boomers born before 1965, no more than 2 percent identify as LGBTQ.

> "I really feel for my transgender friend who told me today that her stepdad said she has to be the 'man' of the house, and this was around the time she was realizing her own dysphoria. That combined with the rest of life being immersed in toxic masculine culture must have made it very difficult for her to come out as trans. It is not surprising that transgender people have so much trauma, being raised in a society that values being 'masculine' as much as it does."

Slowly, diversity is becoming more visible and mainstream. I'm thinking of the transgender child in your kid's eighth-grade classroom. The boss at work who is a lesbian woman, married with a wife. The coworker who begins gender transition. The client who is gender-nonconforming and whose appearance—clothing, hair, personal styling—doesn't conform to traditional norms. The

The US National Institutes of Health uses the term *sexual and gender minority populations,* which it defines as including "individuals who identify as lesbian, gay, bisexual, asexual, transgender, two-spirit, queer, and/or intersex. Individuals with same-sex or -gender attractions or behaviors and those with a difference in sex development are also included. These populations also encompass those who do not self-identify with one of these terms but whose sexual orientation, gender identity or expression, or reproductive development is characterized by non-binary constructs of sexual orientation, gender, and/or sex."

> **BDSM** is a term for the consensual power exchange play of bondage and discipline, dominance and submission, and sadism and masochism. It was brought with verve, if not full accuracy, to public attention by E. L. James's *Fifty Shades* trilogy of best-selling books.

neighbors down the street in a long-standing polyamorous relationship. The college guy who shows up at a frat party in red hot pants—just because he likes the look. An old buddy from high school who's thrilled to be a stay-at-home dad. Storytelling in television and film with characters who are gay or trans or nonbinary or asexual—not as tokens, not even with their identity as a plotline in the story, but simply as themselves. The gay couple at the bakery, excited to order their wedding cake. The friend inspired by *Fifty Shades* who enjoys the kinky play of BDSM, instead of what she calls "vanilla" sex. The young person who goes by the gender-neutral pronoun *ze*. And, of course, also in this mix are people not sure how to use an alternative term like *ze* or what it and the rest of these transformations really mean.

Whether you're that guy in the hot pants just wanting to live out a style of masculinity that's true to you or the married lesbian boss just doing your job or the straight heterosexual couple perfectly content with your vanilla sex and traditional gender roles, this new cultural moment offers more freedom and opportunity to live an authentic life.

> "Our generation is more accepting than ever. Being more exposed to different identities allows us to not think of gender the same way our parents and their parents do. It allows us to think outside of the **boy = blue** and **girl = pink** boxes and to start being more positively receptive to different ways of expression."

This cultural shift addresses the contradictory irony from the last chapter about America's founding narrative: that we are the land of the free where we defend individual rights, yet we insist that everyone must adhere to the same narrow set of gender and sexual scripts. The insistence may not feel like a contradiction or a problem if you're someone who is happy with the traditional norms. If you're a heterosexual and cisgender person who is gender-conforming—if you easily fit within that *F* or *M* box, comfortably present to the world as feminine or masculine, and happily follow the standard romance story—then the box won't pinch. But it's a box, nevertheless. It still restricts your room to move. And, in truth, few fit perfectly all their lives into any one box.

At some point, the standard script will feel limiting, or they will fail to live up to its dictates. There will be a time when a man wants to cry without being considered weak, when a woman wants to assert herself without being considered a pushy bitch, when a person wants to simply *be* without gender expectations programming their every move. Pretty much everyone experiences some degree of disapproval or bullying when they don't do their gender right, in accordance with the norms expected by society. In this sense, gender expression is policed. People who violate the norms attract notice; their behavior stands out and is often criticized. To the girl: *Honey, you can't be a tomboy forever.* To the boy: *Don't be a sissy; man up!*

Before the concept of gender and sexual diversity came into the mainstream, many people had to be "in the closet." They had to hide aspects of their gender and sexuality in order to live safe from discrimination and stigma. The pressures of closeting create a difference between what a person understands to be true of themselves and what they can publicly express. To describe this difference, researchers talk about gender in terms of **assignment** (given at birth), **identity** (how a person feels inside), and **expression** (what they present to the world). For a cisgender and gender-conforming person, these three aspects are likely to align (for example, a person assigned female sex at birth who sees herself as a girl/woman and voluntarily follows feminine social norms for behavior and dress). For a transgender, intersex, or gender-nonconforming person, these aspects may not align well at all, causing significant mental stress (or **gender dysphoria**). Similarly, in terms of sexuality, researchers differentiate **desire** or **attraction** from **behavior** and **identity**: a person might experience same-sex desire but not feel safe to act on that desire or to claim it as their public identity.

After the US Supreme Court legalized same-sex marriage in 2015, the White House was lit up in the rainbow colors.

Culture tries to tell us how we must live out our gender and sexuality, but the truth is that gender and sexual identity have *always* been more diverse and complex than the standard scripts allow. From this point of view, these cultural scripts get in the way of people's rights as individuals to decide how to live their lives. The scripts rein in autonomy and agency. If the scripts offer only one option—everyone must be a gender-conforming heterosexual—then they curb individuality. Everyone values their right to personal expression and benefits from flexibility and choice. We don't all have to live out our gender and our consensual sexuality confined to the same tight scripts, shamed and punished if we dare to stray. The scripts can be more accommodating. When people have the freedom to express their gender identity outside the stereotypes assigned to femininity and masculinity, as well as the freedom to express their consensual sexual desires outside mandatory heteronormativity, then a wider and more genuine range of ways to live becomes possible, for *all* of us.

The new gender and sexual revolution claims the right for people to tell their own story, to write their own script—one that is authentic and meaningful to them. I believe that most people are good-intentioned, trying to get through the day and do the right thing, generally happy to let the neighbors do their own thing, aware that people are all different and that's pretty much okay. Most Americans want to live in a society that protects the right of law-abiding residents to live their lives in peace. A strong democracy acknowledges and accommodates this diversity of its members—to the benefit of the group as a whole. Celebrating diversity makes our civic fabric flexible instead of rigid. It makes society more resilient. It helps civil society thrive.

Chapter 7

CONVERSATION, CONSENSUS, AND CULTURAL COMPETENCE

We arrive here at the core values of the Manisexto: full inclusion and equity. Creating a level playing field, where people have a fair and equal chance to participate and flourish. The script about America as the land of opportunity has too often failed to live up to its promise. People are crushed by the notion of meritocracy when they discover it is blockaded from becoming fully real by racism, sexism, and other barriers of privilege.

Going forward in pluralistic America, three elements characterize the potential for this moment of change: conversation, consensus, and cultural competence. These words all share a root through their prefix *co-*, a Latin term that encompasses meanings of "bringing together," "in common," "in union," "jointly," and "equally." We don't all have to think the same way about everything related to this new moment of gender and sexual transformation, but we are bound together in the common good. We do better as a community when we commit to making real the principle of justice for all.

Take the word *conversation*. From the Latin *conversatio*, it has an interesting history; its meaning alters over time from "live with" and "keep

> Guidelines for promoting diversity in community: Make space for conversation. Let people speak who haven't been allowed to tell their story. Practice active and attentive listening. Dismantle unearned privilege. Respect difference.

company with" to "talk with." From this history comes the lesson that shared speech is central to the formation of community. Sometimes the resistance to diversity stems from a concern that it's divisive to talk about our differences. The fear is that by acknowledging difference, we call attention to what separates us in a way that splinters and weakens the group. Yet the opposite is true: to talk about diversity is to talk about community. Making room for such discussion builds social bonds. Diversity is not the source of division or discord. As American poet and civil rights activist Audre Lorde said, "It is not difference that immobilizes us, but silence. And there are so many silences to be broken." Talking about diversity can be difficult, but it can also be easy. Community comes about by including the perspectives of members who have been marginalized in the past, people who have been forced into silence and invisibility. We make a community whole and strong by respecting all voices. The purpose of inclusion is to value—ideally, to delight in—the diversity of voices in conversation with one another.

"It is not difference that immobilizes us, but silence. And there are so many silences to be broken." —Audre Lorde

For too long, mechanisms of shaming enforced silence. People were not allowed to live out their authentic gender and sexual identities. People were not allowed to speak out about their experiences of sexual abuse. Taboos against giving voice to truth kept diversity in the closet and swept sexual wrongdoing under the rug. But these demands for silence only led to the further trauma of victim-blaming ("She was asking for it," "He brought it on himself") and internalized stigma and shame ("There must be something wrong with me"). In a sex-negative culture, such confusion, anxiety, guilt, and fear all conspire to keep people quiet.

"Making teens think that their sexuality is something that is harmful or shameful probably leaves them less likely to be honest and leaves them with guilt."

Ongoing efforts now break through these toxic taboos. Campaigns for the civil rights of sexual and gender minority populations have broken through ambivalence and stonewalling. The #MeToo and #BlackLivesMatter movements break through silence to advocate justice for survivors of sexual assault and racial justice for society. New concepts arise in popular consciousness. People are talking about sex in a more upfront and forthright way. Through conversation within community—public discourse, media coverage, sex education curricula, chats in the workplace and with neighbors—society's sexual scripts open up and evolve. We rethink the interconnection among social justice issues of race, sex, gender, poverty, disability, and more. Truth is spoken.

For this civil dialogue to succeed, it's crucial that we keep talking with one another across differences: those already onboard this cultural shift and those more hesitant about the changes, the progressive and the conservative, the queer pioneer and the gender normative. We're not all going to agree. But democracy doesn't require everyone to agree; far from it. We need lively debate and lots of room for it—along with shared commitment to keep all forms of bigotry out of the discussion. Our job as a society is to talk together as equals about the new range of stories and cultural scripts. Through such open conversation are human rights protected and civil society bolstered.

"I think trans discussions will become less taboo as generations become more and more accepting, aware, and inclusive. I definitely think it is a work in progress, but it is a fight worth fighting for, even if there are some feelings of confusion or disagreement."

As more people are allowed to tell their story, a new *consensus* emerges. It's another resonant *co-* word, from the Latin verb *consentire*, "to agree," itself derived from *con-* and *sentire*, meaning to "feel together." A consensus signals that as a society we are feeling our way toward a new, updated understanding. It was only in 1920 that women's national voting rights were established in the US. Only in 1967 that interracial marriage became a legal option throughout America (in the adorably named *Loving v. Virginia* Supreme Court case that barred white-supremacy miscegenation laws). At the time, many people found both of those prospects disturbing. Gradually, we changed our minds. Today, no one seriously suggests repealing women's suffrage or once again outlawing interracial marriage. We reached a new consensus.

> "I'm still not really out because with my religious family I have to be careful, so the queer community online has been a saving grace for me. I'm not really sure about my sexuality but I know I'm not straight and I hope that one day I will be a lot more comfortable with myself! I wish I could change my parents' homophobia, but I can't see that ever happening so at some point I am just going to have to start living my truth."

Here's another example: Used to be, we forced left-handed kids to write and draw with their right hand. Schools forbade left-handedness. Christianity even associated it with the devil. Society stigmatized it, with bias embedded in language (*gauche*, as the French word for *left*, means "vulgar and tacky"; *sinister*, as the Latin word for *left*, means "creepy and evil"; to "have two left feet" is to be clumsy). Now, left-handedness is normalized. We recognize it as a genetically influenced natural variation occurring in about 10 percent of the population, not as a bad choice or a nasty inclination—and certainly not as a matter of morality. We accommodate it, with left-handed scissors and desks at school for the kids. Mainly, we just ignore it, as a nonissue. We let people be. That's one hopeful vision of where society is headed, once we more fully integrate the changes of the new gender and sexual revolution. Heterosexual kids have never had to come out to their parents as straight, and one day we can imagine the same will be true of kids who aren't heterosexual. We'll support young people's development and let them be, one way or the other. Left-handed or right-handed, gay or straight. A future free of homophobia.

Times are changing in this inclusive cultural transformation. Society is less disturbed by diversity and more supportive of equal rights. Some people continue to find nontraditional modes of sexuality and gender to be problematic—that it is unacceptable to live as a lesbian woman, a gay man, a trans person, or as someone who is gender nonconforming. But, as we've noted, that demographic of protest steadily shrinks. Without concurring on all the details, the public is beginning to consent to a wider set of cultural scripts. What the ultimate implications of these changes are, time will tell. I, for one, am hopeful—and thankful—for a growing cultural zeitgeist that allows people to live authentic lives and that draws a hard line against sexual misconduct.

> "I can't help but wonder how many people were closeted for all of their lives because they were scared of how society would react towards them. How many would thrive in today's society based on the wider range of acceptance through the media?"

Here's the third *co-* term relevant to the discussion: *competence*. Latin again, referencing the capacity to deal adequately with something, from *com-* "together" and *petere* "to aim at, go toward, seek." A valuable skill nowadays is the capacity to seek cultural competence about gender and sexual diversity. Behind cultural competence is the category of necessary knowledge, the idea that there are things everyone needs to know to function well. No matter what one's opinion might be about these conversations and emerging consensus around inclusion, life in twenty-first-century America now *requires* a certain degree of familiarity and comfort with diversity. Despite the backlash, enough has been gained that there is no going back to narrower and more repressive models for how sexuality and gender must be lived. A central question in America today is how to incorporate and live out this new norm. The issue becomes one of cultural competence.

The etymology of **homophobia** refers literally to the fear of homosexual people; more broadly, along with **transphobia**, the terms refer to prejudice against people who are gay, lesbian, bisexual, or transgender. In the past, these identities have carried **stigma**, or negative stereotypes and biased feelings. Stigma is enacted in society as discrimination. Over time, it can be internalized by the person being stigmatized, if they believe that the biased viewpoints are correct and the discrimination justified. Such internalized stigma is a significant public health problem, as it can lead to low self-esteem, lack of self-acceptance, acting out, and associated mental health issues of anxiety and depression.

Having cultural competence means that a person functions effectively and ethically in diverse settings and recognizes the social value of inclusion and equity. Wrapped up in the history of American white supremacy is the fact that the land has always been one of multicultural diversity, with its First Nations ancestral settlement, European colonialism, African slavery, and centuries of worldwide immigration. Today, in order to be a competent citizen ready to work and thrive in the pluralistic and global society of the twenty-first century, a person needs to be comfortable with human diversity across the fullest range of social identity: diversity of race, ethnicity, age, class, dis/ability, size, gender, sexuality, and more. We all need at least a minimum degree of such cultural competence in our workplaces, social media, schools, communities, and homes. We all need awareness. We need knowledge of today's more open contemporary terrain, enough understanding to negotiate with grace and wit the emerging contours of our brave new world.

The notion of cultural competence highlights the fact that respect for equity and inclusion not only strengthens civil society but aids the individual as well. Such competence is to your benefit. Be pragmatic about it, if you want. You will be a more employable worker and a more successful human being—you will have a career advantage and be more socially adept—to the extent that you can move with ease within the gender and sexual diversity of contemporary society and know how to act in accordance with the bedrock importance of affirmative consent in all your intimate relationships. You'll be really clear about what constitutes sexual harassment and discrimination, so you don't screw up and hurt someone—including yourself and your own career. From this perspective, cultural competence is sometimes called "future proofing" our workplaces.

> "I joined this class to become more accepting of different types of people. I was not necessarily transphobic, but transsexuals didn't seem natural and deep down they made me a little uncomfortable. This class changed my mind."

None of this is meant to encourage a shallow commitment to cultural competence or a mercenary attitude of hypocrisy toward it. That's the downside—if promoting the notion means people think it's enough to merely talk the talk but not walk the walk. Competence can mask the lack of deeper support for principles of diversity.

Remember, the goal isn't just to look competent, so as to check off the box on the mandatory workplace diversity training. The goal is to become genuine champions of full inclusion and equity.

Chapter 8

THE MEANINGS OF QUEER

Here's a confession: I have some reservations about the designation LGBTQIA+.

The abbreviation is sometimes referred to, in a rather derogatory fashion, as an "alphabet soup." Admittedly, the term can be awkward. Its form is inconsistent, with more or fewer letters used in different contexts to represent a range of identities but with a general trend toward an ever-growing string of initials. The biggest drawback, however, is that LGBTQIA+ represents a minority-rights approach that might miss out on a bolder and ultimately more transformative effort at social justice.

Let me explain. If the problem is the denial or exclusion of the range of diversity around gender and consensual sexuality, then two potential remedies exist. In the first approach, we can use versions of the term LGBTQIA+ to talk about sexual and gender minority populations and to aim for full inclusion. The purpose of the letters is to literally spell out the array of diversity that characterizes us as humans. We are not all cisgender and gender-conforming heterosexuals: *cis-het*, in the shorthand. The "alphabet soup" brings to the table those minority identities that the traditional cultural scripts have ignored or stigmatized. This approach increases visibility and forges community. It creates safe space for people to live fuller and more authentic lives. Its goals are education and advocacy for the protection of minority rights. LGBTQIA+ activism, carried out for decades now, addresses head-on the problems of heteronormativity and homophobia. This activism has secured important civil rights successes such as marriage equality, and it fuels annual community celebrations such as Gay Pride parades, rollicking along worldwide under the rainbow flag.

In support of this notion of diversity, some people identify themselves as *queer* and as part of the *queer community*, using the term as a catch-all umbrella for the LGBTQIA+ abbreviation. While queer was originally intended as an insult, activists and academics have reclaimed the slur to signal an unashamed life lived outside traditional norms for gender and heterosexuality. They use it in self-reference to neutralize the hate speech by calling into question the need to conform: *Yeah, I'm queer and I don't fit the norms, but I'm okay with that and know I'm a good person; it's society that needs to change.*

Against the notable political advantages of this minority-rights approach weigh certain disadvantages. Yes, the approach gives voice and makes space for diversity, but it does so at a cost. It fights for rights at the cost of continuing the division between the sexual and gender minority population that is seeking inclusion and the already-sanctioned majority population that holds such rights. The abbreviation LGBTQIA+ and its various forms maintain the separation of this minority from the majority, the non-normative from the normative, the queer from the non-queer, the margin from the mainstream. The approach maintains a narrative about an outsider group seeking admission to the charmed circle of those power-wielding, gender-conforming, cis-het insiders.

> "It feels like when we put labels on groups of people, we isolate them. By labeling a group of people, we say that they are different. We are defining them. They become a person that is not the same as me."

From the minority standpoint, of course, it's not the LGBTQIA+ term that is shunting anyone off into a rainbow ghetto. It's the reality of discrimination itself that creates this division, as anyone knows who's had slurs flung at them—*queer, fag, dyke, slut, whore, bitch, pervert, pussy, sissy*: all terms of hate speech for someone not doing their sex or gender right. The divisiveness is enforced by the group with power acting from a self-serving instinct to maintain its privilege by holding itself superior over others it deems less worthy.

There exactly is the risk of the minority-rights approach: it permits the majority to continue holding itself separate. It enables this majority, for whom the model fits, to rest in a comfortable, self-satisfied fiction that "this gender and sexual diversity stuff has nothing to do with us." It may even allow them off the hook. All the majority need do is perform what feels like a benevolent act of largesse—allow a Pride festival in the community, hire a lesbian mom at work, or accommodate a transgender teen at the high school—to dust off their hands and conclude, "We've done our part." But tolerance is not enough. It is not true inclusion. Its limited effect sidesteps a deeper commitment to equity. Ultimately, tolerance fails as a real game-changer.

> "Everyone wants to be accepted in some kind of way."

The Manisexto moves beyond mere tolerance. It espouses a bolder approach, more capacious and inclusive, to reframe the conversation: not as one of merely securing rights for sexual and gender minority populations but as recognizing the diversity that characterizes us all, so as to normalize difference and eliminate the twisted logic of separation that denied rights in the first place. Gender identity and sexual identity are diverse, and that's *normal*.

The shift is an important one. This second approach highlights the unifying fact of diversity itself. Not everyone is or needs to be the same. There is no stigma to difference. The truth is we all form part of the rich diversity of human identity and expression. A minority identity that does not fall within a society's *norm*, defined as statistical average, still falls within its moral norm, defined as the society's regulatory standards of appropriate behavior. As with the earlier discussion of left-handedness, an identity may be statistically less common but still fully part of the normal and moral diversity of ways to be human. *Normal* expands here into a wider and more inclusive category. Because humans are diverse in so many ways, across so many descriptors of identity, this approach centers diversity itself as the norm, instead of centering cis-het as the norm.

From this perspective, the alphabet soup abbreviation may come to include even more letters, added on to represent the mainstream or "vanilla"
varieties of gender and sexuality: *H* for heterosexual, *C* for cisgender, *S* for
straight—so many letters that the notion of abbreviation collapses and
what emerges instead is a glorious full-spectrum rainbow. Looked at this
way, a man who is cisgender, heterosexual, and traditionally masculine is
just as rainbow-hued as a transgender man or a butch lesbian woman or
someone who is non-binary or polyamorous or asexual.

RuPaul, Emmy-award-winning TV producer, famously said, "We're all born naked, and the rest is drag."

It's important to emphasize that the heterosexual mainstream majority
does *not* need more space or representation in the culture, so this move is
not intended to crowd out the minority by co-opting queer space. Putting
that cis-het dude under the rainbow flag backfires if it only serves to rein-
force his privilege and push marginalized groups further to the edges. The
intention isn't to dismiss the particularity of LGBTQIA+ lives and gloss
over the history of discrimination. It's like the problem of defensively saying "All lives matter" in response to the #BlackLivesMatter movement:
of course all lives matter, but that rejoinder ignores the specific minority
experience of racism. The point is for recognition of the fullest diversity
that encompasses both minority and majority populations together, both
margins and center. Positive sexuality includes all forms of consensual sexuality and gender identity. As this fact of diversity is recognized and normalized, discrimination lessens, inclusion occurs, and equity takes hold.

RuPaul, the Emmy-award-winning drag queen and TV producer of
RuPaul's Drag Race, famously said, "We're all born naked, and the rest is
drag." From childhood onward, we all learn to perform gender and sexuality in accordance with the scripts that our culture deems acceptable. The
scripts come complete with costuming we put on—color-coded from birth
as pink for girls and blue for boys and differentiated throughout life as
women's wear versus men's wear. We all learn to "do drag." As we enact
these social scripts—and as some of us push back against them—questions
emerge: about the necessity of these rules of behavior, about how they are

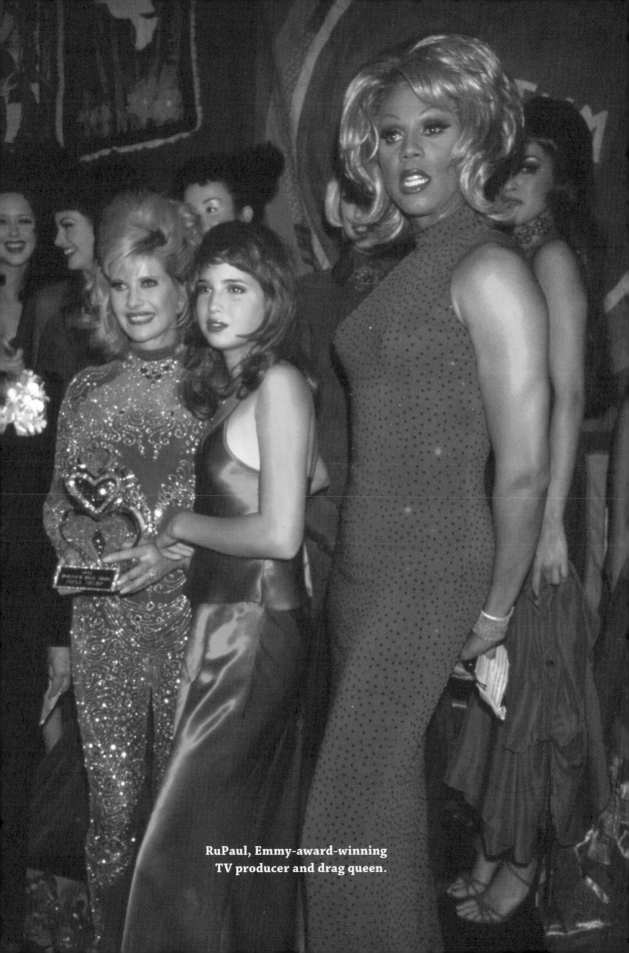

RuPaul, Emmy-award-winning
TV producer and drag queen.

policed through stigma and shaming, about what gets approved as normative and why, about who gets kept out of that charmed circle and why.

In this sense, someone can identify as queer who is "queering"—posing
a query, casting doubt on—these standard rules about how one is supposed to live out gender and sexuality. This definition of *queer* as "to question, to ask, to try to find out" stems from an ancient lineage and links to
the etymology of the Latin-derived verb *inquire*. According to the *Oxford
English Dictionary*, it's the oldest meaning attached to the word *queer*, with
examples dating back to the fourteenth century. A person might call themselves queer as a way of questioning the norm, to make a point that not
everyone fits—or needs to fit—inside neat and binary boxes of male versus
female, masculine versus feminine, straight versus gay. To make the point
that people can live moral and fulfilling lives beyond these binaries. That
one need not conform to an ideal about what is proper simply because it
is traditional. That there is value in going against the grain and thinking
outside the box. In this same sense, a person might identify as transgender who is seeking to transform the imperatives that culture assigns to
gender. As gender theorist Kate Bornstein writes, "Anyone who wants to
question or study gender is transgressing gender. I think anyone who has
either the desire or the courage to own their transgressions against gender
is transgender."

> "We should not be thinking about just male and
> female, and pink and blue, but should be thinking
> about the many other things that make us
> who we are."

As a professor, I teach that the purpose of higher education is precisely
this mode of critical inquiry: to question fundamental assumptions and
probe toward deeper understanding. Instructors and students are supposed to query incessantly into everything. What we think we know, the
status quo of knowledge, may not be correct. Copernicus and Galileo stand
as paradigmatic examples: the sun doesn't rotate around the Earth, despite
commonsense observation and the insistence of the highest authorities of
the time. From this perspective, the university can be seen as the queerest
of our cultural institutions. We form a wondrously queer community of

unruly new knowledge and radical possibility—one where I want all my students to feel centered and affirmed.

Here is the argument pushed to its furthest horizon: we may all be queer, in this sense of posing questions about gender and sexuality. We can be *queer-minded* whether or not we identify our gender or sexuality as queer. The point isn't whether desire is same-sex or opposite-sex, whether one is transgender or cisgender. The point is to challenge the one-size-fits-all requirement of uniformity. The point is to undermine unearned privilege within a society's power structure, in order to open up more space for more people. Here, queer is tied not to identity but to a way of thinking. This usage clarifies that the problem isn't the box or the mainstream, per se—obviously, there's nothing wrong with being heterosexual or cisgender or gender-conforming, when that's your authentic self. The problem is an insistence that everyone must steer their boat down that same mainstream or be lost. For too long have we been taught that the mainstream—the malestream—alone floats the Good Ship. Envision instead a branching river delta of boating pleasures!

To be queer in this way is what anyone can do who cares about freedom of thought and the values of traditional liberal arts education. This vision of diversity applies to everyone committed to consensual sexuality, no matter where they stand on the spectrum: young or old; straight or not; married or not; sexually active or not; trans or cis; girlie-girl feminine, macho-manly, gender non-conforming, or anywhere in between.

All of humanity under the rainbow flag? The new gender and sexual revolution speaks to everyone.

It makes us all into champions of full inclusion and equity.

Chapter 9

SEX IS NOT EVERYTHING

*The Surprising Lesson of Asexuality as
Part of Diversity*

One last point clarifies what it means to champion sex-positive inclusion: as sexual diversity is normalized, sexuality does not need to become more central to the culture; ironically, it may become less so. The more the culture makes room for sexual diversity, the less prominent sexuality can become. Ultimately, there's no need to *celebrate* sexual diversity, simply to ensure equity in its regard. Another way to put the point: after the new gender and sexual revolution, neither sex nor gender need be a big deal.

The point highlights the lingering American paradox of sex as overblown while at the same time ignored. The pop culture trades in sex nonstop—songs, billboards, fashion spreads, the latest reality TV show—at the same time that serious discussion of the subject is largely taboo. Parents are too embarrassed to talk with kids about good sex. Schools struggle to teach it. Men's sexuality is excused as biologically driven and outside their control. Women's desire is silenced and shamed even as their bodies are fetishized as sexual objects. Sex is everywhere, but open discussion of good sex is almost nowhere. By dealing with positive sexuality in a meaningful manner—through an insistence on fully informed consent and by accepting sexual and gender diversity through genuine practices of equity and inclusion—the incessant drumbeat of toxic sexuality can go away. The paradox can resolve.

Something that helps get us to this vision of sexual well-being is the new and growing asexuality movement. It's a movement that has been gaining more representation in popular culture and the media. The concept of *asexuality*, understood in a couple of different ways, aids in resolving this toxic paradox of sex as too much but not enough.

Asexuality (or nonsexuality) is an underrecognized identity on the sexual diversity spectrum, although it was documented by Alfred Kinsey, the famous mid-twentieth-century sexuality studies researcher from Indiana University, at rates of around 1 percent for men and women. An asexual person is someone who has no intrinsic desire to have sexual relationships or who experiences only low levels of sexual attraction. This absent or low sexual desire is not because of hormone imbalance, medical condition, or past experience of sexual trauma—all of which can impact sex drive and can be addressed and treated—but simply because asexuality is the person's sexual identity or orientation.

Asexuality is distinct from voluntary abstinence (where someone may have interest in engaging in sexual activity but doesn't act on it) or intentional celibacy (as practiced, for example, by a monk, nun, or priest who takes a religious vow). Being asexual does not mean you are uninterested in human connection. Asexual people can enjoy close friendships and romantic relationships, still falling in love and making a long-term commitment but without a sexual component to the companionship: affection, respect, and bonding, but no erotic longing or consummation. (There are asexual romance novels now appearing in bookstores—check them out!) Some asexual people do choose to engage in sexual activity despite the lack of libido, due to reasons such as desire to please a partner, curiosity, or the wish for children.

> An asexual person is someone who has no intrinsic desire to have sexual relationships or who experiences only low levels of sexual attraction. "Ace" is sometimes used as a shorthand or umbrella term for the asexual community and the various forms of asexuality.

This explanation is one way to understand the significance of asexuality: as an identity that describes how some people relate to sexuality. This identity forms part of the normal diversity spectrum of human sexuality. The asexuality movement of education and advocacy works to increase visibility and inclusion for this group of people and to reduce their experience of marginalization and stigma, just as advocacy does for other minority populations. Asexuality is a way to point out that, for some people, sex is not the big deal the rest of the culture makes it out to be, and that's okay. *Sex is not everything.*

> Activist David Jay founded the Asexual Visibility and Education Network in 2001. Ace Week is now celebrated every October in cities around the world, to promote awareness and acceptance. #Asexual, #AceCommunity, #AceAwareness

A second way to understand the asexuality movement is as a means of saying that for everyone, society as a whole may make too big a deal out of sexuality, in that toxic too-much-but-not-enough way.

What if the sex-positive movement just feels like more pressure? Yes, it opens up space in the culture for people to experience and explore their sexuality within consensual relationships, safe from discrimination, sexist double standards, and shaming. Its guidance is all to the good—to the very good, even. But what if this freshly opened space imposes a new sense of imperative and fuels its own anxiety? What if this new spirit of affirmation feels like bias toward Eros as proof of life lived right: big, bold, sexy, and grand? One more thing you're supposed to master on the checklist of personal empowerment and liberation, when your to-do list is already brimming? What if you like sex fine enough when the moment is right but resent any mandated cultural script to perform or participate in a style that isn't your own? How can you make clear you're simply not interested, without a woman risking labels of tease or prude or a guy being shamed as not man enough, when masculinity is still defined through sexual prowess?

Sex is not everything, and it doesn't have to be your thing. As I've noted, sex-positive does *not* mean "pro-sex," as in you're supposed to be having hot wild sex all the time. There is no mandate to perform sexiness. But the culture can certainly make it feel that way. Asexuality activist David Jay explains this point: "Sexuality has become a thing that everyone is expected to articulate, to experience, and to express publicly. . . . What we want is for people to be able to explore sexuality on their own terms . . . it is about self-discovery and finding what works for you."

This countermessage of "sex is not everything" balances out the weight of sex pushed as overblown cultural messaging. The newly prominent asexual movement comes to play a different role here, not only to recognize and affirm those who experience little or no sexual desire, but also as cultural critique and corrective. Asexuality becomes a way to raise questions about hypersexualization, to talk about unhealthy or coercive elements of sexuality in society. Cultural scripts about both sex and romantic love become oppressive if and when the culture presents them as compulsory. Romance is by no means the only pathway to a happy and fulfilled life. Romantic love, when it occurs, does not need to include sex. And not everyone needs to be hot-pantingly sexual.

The media, pop culture, and the consumer realm can certainly be too sex-saturated. The predominance of sexual imagery and reference can feel oppressive, like possibility is being shut down, not opened up. A cheap and easy default to sexualized near-nudity in advertising—but the bodies all look the same. Young teens left to figure out their burgeoning sexuality— but without the benefit of egalitarian and comprehensive sex education (sexy thongs marketed to preteen girls, anyone?). Porn, more widely accessible than ever before, but nowhere near to modeling positive sexuality. Boys inculcated into toxic cultural scripts of masculinity that reward guys for the role of sexual player and punish them for daring to sit out—*Man up, dude*—or speak out—*Never rat out a bro*. Women subjected to constant pressure to look "hot"—and to somehow make it look ladylike.

> "As a young woman, I am often angry at the expectations that I feel I must fulfill. Women and their bodies are so policed. We are told what we can and cannot be and are overly controlled. A woman that is 'too sexual' is wild and undesirable, but a woman that shows no sexual interest is prudish and therefore undesirable."

A student once asked me if *virgin* was a bad word; he worried about offending someone by accidently using a derogatory term. Let us be very clear: *virgin* is not a bad word. Virgin-shaming or prude-shaming is just as bad as slut-shaming. The sex-positive message here is that it's fine to be less than fully rah-rah about sex. Not having sex is a great choice, if that's the right choice for you. Waiting until you're ready to have sex, until you're in a relationship that feels right, is a great choice. Not jumping on the Big Sexy Bandwagon is a great choice, when Big Sexy is not a game you care to play. Maybe "sexy" isn't a compelling category for you, you'd like to keep that part of life private, that style of appearance doesn't appeal, or you're just not motivated by all the fuss.

"I now realize college students are not hooking up nearly as much as I thought they were."

This "No, thanks" stance can be hard to pull off, however, especially for young people surrounded by the influence of peers in hookup culture and by the trendsetting super-peer of social media. The field of social norms research demonstrates that people tend to do what they think others are doing—youth, in particular, because they want to fit in. We're motivated by "normative belief," or the perception of how social norms operate within our groups, and take cues for our behavior from how we believe peers typically act. Problem is, we're often wrong; it's easy to misjudge what others are up to, to our own detriment. College students, for example, hold normative beliefs about the risk-taking behavior of their peers that are often exaggerated, in ways that can fuel higher-risk behavior.

As sociologist Lisa Wade, author of *American Hookup: The New Culture of Sex on Campus*, writes, "Students overestimate how much sex their peers are having, and by quite a lot. In fact, today's students boast no more sexual partners than their parents did at their age." It can *feel* like the culture is sexed-up, with pressure on campus from everyone thinking they're supposed to be getting drunk and hooking up—when, in fact, everyone isn't, and when they do, the sex is often awkward and one-sided. Wade reports that one-third of college students abstain from hookup culture and are critical of it. The broad approach to asexuality helps highlight the extent to which people are *not* having sex and how that's perfectly fine. Those who advocate for positive sexuality know that sex is not everything.

The Manisexto's commitment to the rainbow diversity of gender and consensual sexuality—including diversity in levels of sexual interest—is about making sure people have the information, resources, and critical-thinking skills to make decisions for themselves in line with their values, to act fairly toward others, and to stand up for justice and equity.

Affirming this diversity is key to the vision of positive sexuality. But if we really want to end bullying and shaming and exclusion—if we really want good sex, both ethical and pleasurable—there's more work to be done.

A persistent pressure remains around bodies and how they are supposed to look. It's as if the culture has been shouting *SEX!* very loudly but along a very narrow bandwidth. As if sex takes up a whole lot of real estate but offers very little room. There's been an impossible and boring sameness to the bodies.

The new gender and sexual revolution works to widen the bandwidth. It makes for more room.

The next task is to think about bodies, in all their stunning diversity.

Manisexto #3

BODY POSITIVITY

All Bodies Are Good Bodies

Chapter 10

THE NAKED TRUTH

Embracing Body Positivity and Diverse
Ways to Embody Gender

Every revolution has its rallying cry. Here's one of ours, trumpeting via hashtag bullhorn into the modern-day rally ground of social media: Own Your #BellyJelly!

In the gender and sexual revolution of the twenty-first century, not only gender and sexual identity present their ranges of diversity. Bodies, booties, and beauty itself shine in diverse forms, with much more variety than the standard cultural scripts have recognized. Today, the Manisexto declares its commitment to equity and inclusion for *all* bodies.

Declares its commitment to #LoveYourCurves.

Its commitment to #FuckYourBeautyStandards!

> "#BellyJelly is very inspirational and insightful. It gave me the self-esteem to think about how this relates to my own life and to be proud in my own body."

Body positivity, also referred to as body acceptance, is a broad social movement. The concept is adopted and used in various ways by individuals and organizations with a range of agendas, but it is always centered around a common core message: Bodies are all different, and that's okay. Your body

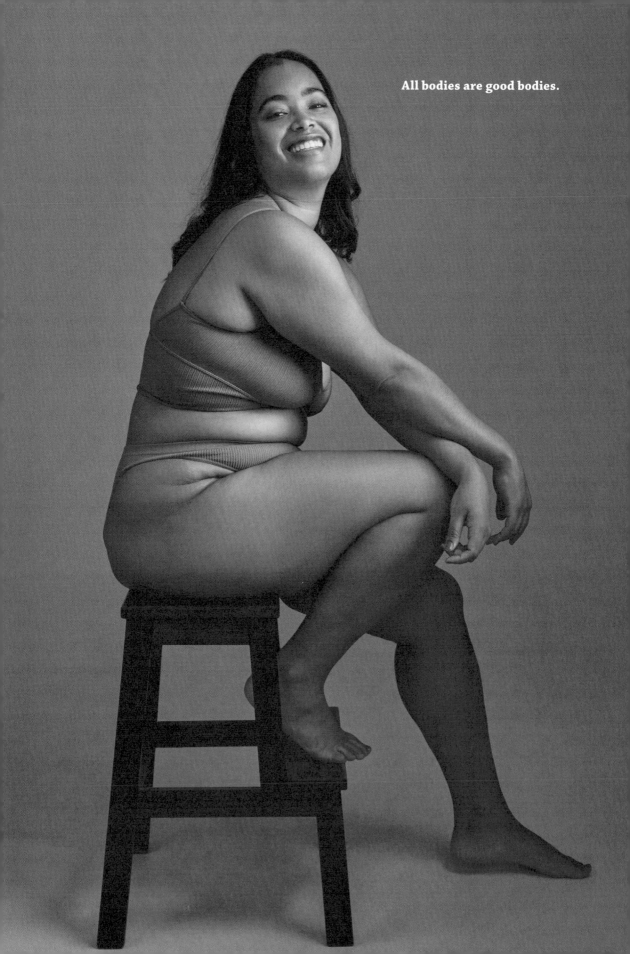

All bodies are good bodies.

does not have to be perfect, in accordance with some impossible cultural ideal. All bodies are good bodies. Here's how one blog writer on a Tumblr website puts it: "A girl doesn't have to be a double zero to be beautiful, a guy doesn't have to have a twelve pack and bulging biceps to be hot."

#LoveYourCurves!

Body positivity often pops up in relation to these discussions of weight and beauty standards, but it actually entails much more. The movement intersects powerfully with efforts around racial justice, anti-ageism, and disability advocacy. Its scope runs so broad precisely because body positivity encompasses all facets of human embodiment: the body's size, shape, skin color, ethnicity, age, and ability status.

Also encompassed is the body's presentation of gender, since so much of gender is about the body. Traditional gender scripts have a *lot* to say about what counts as a good body: pretty of face and curvy for a woman, tall and muscular for a man. These scripts describe—and prescribe—the appropriate way for the body to look, how it should be groomed and clothed and behave, according to whether it is female or male. Here's some shorthand for typical American norms: a real man doesn't wear a skirt, and a lady does not grow bushy underarm hair. We quite literally *embody* gender norms on a regular basis through these rules about how the body is supposed to do its gender right.

But today, there is more social acceptance for people to express their gender in authentic ways, through a broader display of personal styles. The body positive movement frees people from what is needlessly limiting and what can become toxic in these narrow cultural scripts. Nowadays, presentation of gender can be traditionally feminine or masculine but also gender nonconforming, nonbinary, fluid, queer. Central to body positivity is the conviction that there's more than one right way to embody your gender.

"Every body is beautiful and deserves praise."

Body acceptance contributes its power of analysis to the new gender and sexual revolution with three main arguments.

First, society is *lookist*. It has a bias toward the beautiful. People get judged based on their looks, all the time. Society valorizes certain types of bodies, bodies that look a certain way, more so than others. Traditionally, characteristics of the body are organized as value-laden poles of opposites. One pole receives praise, and society rewards bodies that match its shiny epitome of physical perfection. The other pole stands devalued and shamed. These binaries of physicality represent the constant evaluation and judgment that we make about ourselves and others: Is the body slim, or is it fat? Does the physique correspond to the desirable shape, or is it out of shape, the wrong shape? Is the body young, or do wrinkles and sags age it as old? Is it fully abled or marked by disabilities, whether physical or cognitive? Is the skin pale, or is it dark? (Bias in favor of lighter skin tones—what's called "colorism"—can occur both across and within racial ethnic groups.)

This system of preferencing means that the category of the "good body" is socially constructed: what counts as attractive or sexy is shaped by society. These social scripts for the ideal body change over time and vary from place to place. In the twentieth century, for example, American ideals for women's bodies swung back and forth: flat-chested and slim-hipped was all the rage for 1920s flapper gals and during the 1960s Twiggy era, but the curvy 1950s Marilyn Monroe look, as well as that of today, favors an hourglass figure and big booty. What doesn't change, as this pendulum swings, is the fact of a standard and the pressure to conform to it.

Social scripts for the ideal body change over time but not the fact of a standard and the pressure to conform to it.

The second argument of body positivity is that this lookism is not neutral but is fueled by various forms of discrimination. To illustrate this point, I do a live online experiment with my students in class; you can try it too. Type "beautiful body" or "sexy body" into your internet search browser and see what images pop up. Overwhelmingly, what fills the screen are pictures of white, thin, busty, young, scantily clad, able-bodied women. According to Google search algorithms, such is what America counts as the beautiful and sexy body. As you scroll through the images—and as we are all exposed to these incessant visual messages from social media and advertising—the sense emerges: *this* is how a body should look, *that's* the way a body should be.

American ideal of 1920s flappers.

"Growing up as an African American young lady, I had my fair share of struggles with feeling beautiful. I remember in high school, I had to do a project on beautiful women, and I was so discouraged with Google's results. When I searched 'beautiful women,' only Caucasian women popped up. Majority of them were skinny, with long beautiful hair. This was such a hard pill to swallow. I remember being bullied by my classmates because my hair was not as long or as straight as my classmates of other races. I can recall so vividly the emotions I felt as I cried to my mom about not being cute like the other girls."

It's significant that the gender identity coming up in these internet images is that of women. More so than men, women—even very young girls—are judged on the appearance of their bodies (although we'll think a lot more about male bodies in the chapters to come). Women and girls are subjected to an ongoing sense their bodies are there to be looked at, especially by men and boys. Scholars call this the *male gaze*: an omnipresent cultural "eye" whose viewpoint is male and heterosexual. When culture operates from the point of view of this male gaze, it sees women as decorative visual objects existing for the pleasure of the viewer. It's then but a short step to seeing women as sexual objects.

"Us guys don't really have to worry about that; I feel like we are much less pressured to look a certain way, have a certain body type, and conform to this notion of what is attractive."

"Men do not face the same fatphobia that women do. For women, even if you have just a little gut, men will consider you fat. For men, if they have a gut, people will refer to it as a 'dad body' and it is completely acceptable."

"I think a lot of women believe their body to be their only valuable attribute and thus are terrified to lose it. Take for instance the phrase **Shake your money maker**. Women are taught to flaunt their body as a natural-given gift and the only advantage they have (obviously, I disagree with this)."

Within this visual economy of female bodies doing the work of looking good and getting valued, or devalued, based on their physical self-
presentation, women are *supposed* to be beautiful. It's part of the role they're
expected to play in society. Women suffer more than men from these sexist
expectations and the pressures to conform to beauty standards. Poor body
image and body dissatisfaction are rampant among women, with powerful
impacts on self-esteem. One study found almost double the percentage of
US women than men not satisfied with their body. Another study found
that over 90 percent of women preferred a different body shape. Further-
more, researchers report that girls' body unhappiness and their internaliza-
tion of the thin-body ideal begins as young as *three years of age*.

> "One thing I've practiced through my self-work is
> finding something I'm not comfortable doing, like
> going out without makeup, and continuing to do
> it until I feel comfortable. This has done wonders for me.
> I've practiced this with not doing anything to my hair, not
> wearing makeup, wearing clothes that are comfortable
> instead of dressing up. Before, I would not even allow my
> boyfriend to see me unless I had done all of these things,
> but now I get so excited for a date because stressing about
> how I look is no longer a concern."

This gender difference in how men and women experience their bodies
reveals the sexism behind these cultural standards, but other sources of
bias are at work as well. The standards for judging what counts as attractive and sexy grow out of the underlying prejudices of a society. These
prejudices shape a form of desirability politics wherein some people get
labeled as beautiful versus others who are considered, in the harsh language of the dating marketplace, "unfuckable." To the extent that America
remains marked by ableism, ageism, and white supremacy, society continues to accord most value to the fit, abled, youthful, and light-skinned
body. Discrimination against people who are older or disabled means that
the younger body and the fully abled body come to define what counts as
the "good body."

Racism means that beauty standards favor the white body. One result of this inequity is that people of color and racial minority communities can end up internalizing such racism against themselves, fueling the further discrimination of colorism: that preference toward lighter skin and stigma against darker skin. Despite today's successful Black supermodels, performers, and celebrities, the "Black is Beautiful" movement of the 1960s civil rights era still has a way to go in erasing bias toward Euro-American facial features and standards of lighter-toned skin and smooth hair.

"African American women struggle to feel accepted and viewed as beautiful by society when it comes to our hair. Society says the natural texture of our hair isn't cute or professional. So, we had to change our hair and that is why there are so many who wear weaves/wigs all the time."

#LoveYourBody

The larger point is not only that societies discriminate against certain categories of bodies but that these forms of bigotry shape desire itself. Not only beauty is socially constructed—love is too. As Kate Harding, the feminist body-positivity writer and coauthor of *Lessons from the Fat-o-sphere*, says, "Of all the maddening side effects of our narrow cultural beauty standard, I think the worst might be the way it warps our understanding of attraction." What makes us click with one person and not another? We tend to think that these matters of romantic attraction and sexual desire are deeply personal, that love and lust spring from our heart and loins as a particularized expression of our individual psyche. *There is my Cupid's match, my soul mate!* In truth, what counts as our "type" and produces this sense of puzzle pieces fitting together is partly—perhaps largely—shaped by the society we grow up in.

#BlackIsBeautiful

"Once you get to know someone, things like weight and appearance matter less and less. If you've met a guy and he doesn't like you because of your weight or appearance, he isn't worthy of your time or energy anyway. You should want to meet a guy who likes you and wants you for who you are as a person, regardless of what you look like. Those guys are out there."

We internalize society's biases in ways that are limiting and tragic. It's hard to free ourselves completely from this function of what researchers term *implicit bias* or *unconscious bias*. Even when we actively work to uproot negative stereotypes from our thinking and decision-making, it's hard to shake ourselves completely free from such deep-seated influences. The narrow ideal of what counts as good-looking and sexy ends up narrowing who we find to be desirable and who we fall in love with. Perhaps even worse, the narrowness of these ideals harms our own self-image. We internalize impossible notions, judge that we can never match up, and end up feeling we aren't desirable and worthy of love in return. Self-confidence suffers; we feel shame and even self-hate.

"There was this stigma growing up of what it meant
to be a beautiful Black woman. You had to have light
skin, bone-straight hair, a thin waist, and a big ass.
But how does that look to younger Black girls who didn't
have that body growing up? As for myself, I am a plus-size
young woman. I was always afraid of my curves and I had
major anxiety over my stretch marks. I was afraid I would
never find anyone who would love me for me. My mom
always told me I was beautiful, but social media was telling
me different. Now that I am older and more mature, I have
grown to love myself."

In response to these problems of lookism and prejudice, the body positivity movement makes its third argument, one of affirmation linked to an activist call for change: All bodies are good bodies. Love your body. No more shaming or bullying about the perfect body. Time to widen and redefine narrow cultural definitions of attractiveness, sexiness, and gender display.

It's an argument of respect, of full equity and inclusion for all bodies. This affirmation of new and wider notions about what constitutes the good body entails much more than just beauty standards. The movement becomes about racial equity, disability justice, and the end of age discrimination. It widens ideals for body image as it pushes us to think about the beauty of the older body, the differently abled body, the body of color, the gender-queer body.

The impact of this movement is huge. Body positivity is a significant component of the commitment to diversity, equity, and inclusion. The movement is also hugely needed. While it might seem strange to say, it's not easy having a body. Managing our bodies—dealing with the sheer, brutal fact of embodiment—is one of the great challenges of life. Although the body is a site of pleasure and potential, it is also often a site of embarrassment, of limitation, of failure. The body leaks, bleeds, stinks, and oozes. The body bears the violence of others. The body is about restriction, the vulnerability of illness and accident, the indignities and confusion of rapid bodily change during puberty and then again as our bodies age. Ultimately, it's about the tragic inevitability of death.

"While I may not hate my body size or even shape in the same way as most people, as a transgender man I still battle gender dysphoria which affects how I view myself. I understand how it feels to not feel at home within your own skin, and it is a problem I believe every individual deals with to some extent no matter how 'flawless' they may be."

Of all the issues my students and I discuss in class, this one stands out as most universally true: growing up, everyone at some point felt bad about their bodies. Although the guys and girls experience the pressures differently, both still feel them—often intensely. As a child or teen, everyone was made to feel shame by family, peers, or the culture that their body in some way wasn't right, wasn't enough, wasn't as perfect as it should be. Now living as young adults deeply entrenched within the visual culture of social media, these students find the message of body positivity to be affirming. But the messages are complex and can even seem contradictory or ripe for misunderstanding.

"People should take pride in their bodies and love what they have without feeling pressure from others."

Here is the first misunderstanding: the movement does not grant license to abandon the important duty to look after your body. In fact, the very core of its message is *self-care*.

Chapter 11

BODY POSITIVITY DOESN'T MEAN "LET THEM EAT CAKE!"

It's about Holistic Well-Being

Although body acceptance is not just about weight, the movement's most visible form does often revolve around issues of physical shape. The movement spends much of its energy pushing back against cultural forces that constantly value the body through measurements of BMI, pounds, and clothing size. That's not surprising, as a focus on weight stigma is where this social movement began.

Contemporary body positivity took root in 1960s-era activism around fat acceptance. In 1967, a group of activists staged a "Fat-In" in New York City's Central Park to protest discrimination against people of size; they carried food and banners ("Buddha Was Fat!") and burned diet books. By 1969, principles of body positivity manifested in the founding of the National Association to Advance Fat Acceptance (NAAFA), now the premier fat-rights organization in the country. NAAFA works as a nonprofit public education and advocacy group to unashamedly reclaim and shift the meaning of the term *fat*—like gay rights activists did with *queer*—from a shame-filled insult into a neutral descriptor or term of pride.

> "All throughout my childhood and most of high school, I was always bigger than most girls in my grade. After I lost a lot of weight going into senior year, I received very different treatment from my peers. People were nicer to me, and people that never acknowledged me started to talk to me. I would have never thought losing weight would show people's fatphobia, but it did. Now, even though I know my boyfriend loves me, it is still hard to be fully confident in myself."

From these historical roots, and from common ground shared with the "Black is Beautiful" cultural critique, body acceptance grew. One branch developed into an innovative academic field of inquiry within the humanities and social sciences. Today, *fat studies* is an area of scholarship characterized by strong intersectional and interdisciplinary analysis, with academics exploring the interplay of fat stigma with racism, homophobia, ableism, ageism, and capitalism in the culture's scripts about the good body.

While academia provides the movement with depth of research, what really allowed body positivity to take off was the growth of the internet as an omnipresent global network in the mid-1990s. With the rise of social media platforms since the 2010s, body positivity has expanded rapidly. Social media's massive popularity and impact meant

Important texts from fat studies dazzle with nuanced analysis, such as best-selling author Roxane Gay's *Hunger: A Memoir of (My) Body* (2017); sociologist Sabrina String's *Fearing the Black Body: The Racial Origins of Fat Phobia* (2019); gender studies professor Jason Whitesel's *Fat Gay Men: Girth, Mirth, and the Politics of Stigma* (2014); cultural geographer Julie Guthman's *Weighing In: Obesity, Food Justice, and the Limits of Capitalism* (2011); and American studies scholar Amy Erdman Farrell's *Fat Shame: Stigma and the Fat Body in American Culture* (2011).

that messages of self-acceptance and self-love could easily reach a diverse audience. Body positivity has thrived in particular on platforms that are photo-based. Sites such as Instagram, with over a billion users worldwide, let people post pictures of themselves and connect with others in lively and empowering communities. Last time I clicked on Instagram's #BodyPositive hashtag, I got almost *eighteen million* posts, with more added all the time. Users dub this online space the "Fatosphere," where bloggers and virtual advocacy groups engage in supportive conversation and destigmatize big bodies.

"One influencer that has really made an impact is rising TikTok star Sienna Gomez. She posted a joke video on her account poking fun at today's beauty standard. She danced weirdly and showed off her stomach in a not perfectly flat state. Overnight, she gained millions of views. The best part about Sienna is she's only sixteen. She isn't some adult or older wiser human trying to teach youth. Having girls like Sienna promoting this idea of loving your body is extremely important in this day, because it can be so hard for both girls and boys growing up, watching all these 'perfect people' in the media, to love themselves as they are."

Influencers, including plus-sized celebrities and models, have led body positivity's online presence. Instagram star and eating-disorder survivor Megan Crabbe, better known as @BodyPosiPanda, has 1.3 million followers and blogs regularly about "BoPo." The British-Jamaican plus-sized model Sonny Turner has 300,000 Instagram followers and uses the tagline "Nobodies perfect." Tess Holliday—a body-positive activist and plus-sized model with 2.4 million followers—launched the site #EffYourBeautyStandards ("Fuck your beauty standards") in 2013 as a way to reject the toxic hierarchy that ranks some bodies as more desirable and attractive than others. (Holliday appeared on the cover of *People* magazine in 2015 with the rather fetishizing line "The World's First Size 22 Supermodel!") In 2016, Ashley Graham made news as the first plus-sized model to appear on the cover of *Sports Illustrated*'s annual swimsuit magazine.

While these pressures around the body especially target women, also affected are men. Guys fall under their own set of cultural demands to embody a certain physique. The ideal is to be tall, with very little fat and lots of muscles—especially that iconic six-pack of rippling abs topped by well-developed pecs and bulging bicep "guns." (It's a chilling word usage, in its association of muscularity with violence.) For example, American actor Matt McGorry posted on Instagram about his "big, soft belly" and the difficulty of growing up in "a world that hates fat people and men who are soft, physically and emotionally." He noted perceptively how men are supposed to be "hard and angular, like chiseled impenetrable statues" and how a "lean and muscular physique is the prize of self-control."

> "Men, just like women, can develop eating disorders which are extremely dangerous, yet talked about way less pertaining to men. The pressure to look a certain way leads a lot of people down an unhealthy path."

> "How are body pressures different for men and women? Women are expected to be skinny, but also curvy, but also super fit, and also wear sexy dresses and heels and makeup, while also being proper and lady-like. On the flip side, men are expected to be tall and muscular and macho super-buff and have abs and a good tan, while not showing their emotions, because that somehow makes them less manly."

Researchers term the internalized desire to build muscle mass the "drive for muscularity." They link it to what appear to be rising rates among men of exercise addiction, fueled by the anxiety that their body isn't big and buff enough, even among men with significant musculature. This anxiety condition is called "muscle dysmorphia" or "bigorexia," in contrast to the anorexia that more often affects women. The obsession with muscularity parallels changes in media and cultural ideals for men's bodies: even male action figures (what are called "dolls," if you're a girl) are burlier than they used to be in decades past.

Guys fall under their own set of cultural demands to embody a certain physique.

Body positivity's support for size diversity can, however, lead the movement to be misunderstood. Just as being sex-positive does not mean you're supposed to be having hot, wild sex all the time or there's something wrong with you, being body-positive does not mean you're supposed to be fat. It's not *Let them eat cake!* There's no encouragement to obesity or to an out-of-shape body. The movement is not saying, "Bonbons all day long and never get off the couch." (Although I have been there on that couch, and it does sometimes feel deliciously, delectably, exactly right.) The point of size-positivity is not to argue that anyone *needs* to be overweight. The point is that no

The drive for muscularity can lead to muscle dysmorphia or bigorexia.

one should be discriminated against *because* of their body weight. The point is that fat-phobia, fat-hating, and fat-shaming are all wrong; they can do as much damage, if not more so, than carrying extra pounds. The point is to reduce stigma around obesity and fight the cultural obsession with dieting and gym routines, in order to free people from hatred of their own bodies, all the while encouraging wellness through a holistic approach to physical, mental, and emotional well-being.

"Especially for me because I'm a very tall and skinny guy, I've struggled with how am I not bigger even with doing workouts and sports. For most guys, this happens. You get that enviousness of having the perfect body."

> "It is *confidence* that matters."

A related initiative is promoted by the Association for Size Diversity and Health through their trademarked phrase "Health at Every Size," based on a 2008 book by that title published by Dr. Lindo Bacon, a physiologist and nutritionist who advocates for "body respect." The central idea of #HealthAtEverySize is that "well-being and healthy habits are more important than any number on the scale." A combination of biomarkers and lifestyle factors such as blood pressure, heart rate, levels of stress, social support networks, frequency of enjoyable exercise, and quality of sleep are collectively more important than the measurement of body weight taken in and of itself. Fat gets wrongly used as a proxy for ill health, a misleading oversimplification. If you're slim, you're praised as healthy; if you're overweight, you're condemned as unhealthy. But reality is more complex. A person, for example, could be thin because they're a drug addict or undergoing cancer treatments. Low body weight doesn't necessarily equate with well-being. Thinness doesn't guarantee health. The cult of thinness has in fact fueled dangerous eating disorders affecting mainly young women such as bulimia and anorexia, the deadliest of the mental health conditions and one of the most resistant to treatment.

> "Dating and meeting guys when you aren't fully comfortable in your body is hard for anyone. I struggled for about five years with anorexia and bulimia in which I thought I was big, and now that I have recovered mentally, I am aware of how underweight I am and am self-conscious about being too skinny or boney or my lack of boobs or a butt from having lost too much weight."

While medical research does strongly link obesity to chronic health problems such as heart disease, high blood pressure, diabetes, and some cancers, it is also true that research studies repeatedly find a high failure rate for dieting in which people tend over time to regain the pounds they lose. Fat acceptance suggests the problem is that diets are motivated more by stigma around weight than by a real focus on holistic health. The diet industry, the grooming products industry, the muscle-building industry of food supplements and gym routines: these all feed on people's anxieties about their bodies. They amplify fat-phobic messaging in society and are often designed more to part people from their money than to foster a culture of healthy relationship to the body. Instead of campaigns, for example, against child obesity that focus directly on weight loss, children's public health campaigns could focus on fun exercise, access to the outdoors, nutrition support programs, and the reduction of childhood poverty. The body positive argument here is that the best overall health outcomes result from aiming for wellness at every stage of life and at every size of the body—by encouraging balanced eating and enjoyable physical activity—coupled with a sociocultural approach that addresses fat stigma and structural barriers to health.

> "A person should love and embrace the body they have and try to work out on ways to keep it healthy and lively. By maintaining a positive attitude towards the body, one can live a healthy life full of love and compassion."

Making peace with your body is healthier than gaining and losing weight in an endless cycle of yo-yo dieting. Accepting how your body looks at the stage of life you find yourself is healthier than hating yourself because of your muffin tops or because you can't get your abs flat. Don't torture yourself about needing to exercise in order to "look good." Exercise for your own sense of well-being, for the pleasure of the endorphin rush or the feel of sun on your face as you walk in the fresh air—but not just to lose weight or gain muscle mass. Recognize that everyone's body changes throughout their life span. A woman who's birthed kids will have a broadened waist and hips with stretch marks traced across her belly, and "dad bods" similarly tend to soften and spread and sag throughout the years, as muscle tone and skin elasticity change with age. Such a body is not less beautiful; its beauty simply manifests in a different and more mature form.

While body positivity began with the emphasis on fatness, the movement's focus on size and shape—belly rolls, cellulite, back fat, and stretch marks—has expanded into a wider critique of cultural scripts about the body and an inclusive ethic of self-care. Healthy bodies follow from a healthy society built upon principles of justice and equity, where society values diversity and enables access to health care and economic opportunity. Healthy bodies thrive when families and individuals are supported in their ability to practice self-care.

> "Being comfortable in your body is one of the most important things."

The body positive movement becomes about feeling comfortable with your relationship to your body and how you choose to present that body to the world. The message becomes that it's more important to *feel good* within a society committed to *doing good* than it is to force-fit yourself into any narrow definition of how to *look good*.

Chapter 12

IT'S NOT ABOUT "LOOKING GOOD" BUT ABOUT FEELING GOOD—AND THAT INCLUDES YOUR GENITALS TOO

Looking good is a double-edged sword in the world of body positivity. One popular saying within the movement is the egalitarian insistence that all bodies are beautiful, but just as popular is a sneering dismissal of the whole concern: why does anyone need to worry about being beautiful? During the coronavirus pandemic, the fashion industry experienced a precipitous collapse, with a 79 percent decline in clothing sales. The one item that sold well, with an 80 percent increase? Sweatpants. Maybe a positive aspect of the virus was that it freed us from some of these anxieties of the visual economy. Don't worry so much about how you look. Just be comfortable. Wear what you want, whatever makes you happy and helps you feel good.

> "Being able to see a normal, un-Photoshopped body is so important for young adults." #AllBodiesAreGoodBodies

The dynamic home that body positivity has crafted for itself online has this ironic downside: because so much of social media is based on a visual culture that emphasizes looks, social media often makes body anxiety worse. My students talk about the stress and shame they feel scrolling their Insta feed, flipping through bikini pics or body-building workouts. They describe the temptation to use the tools of online enhancement filters to "fix" their perceived flaws, since the mere existence of these filters intensifies that visual pressure. If you can make yourself look better through a few taps or swipes of the screen, and other people are doing so, why not do it? In fact, one recent study found that 90 percent of young women use a filter or edit their photos before posting online.

> "In the last year or so, I fell victim to the app Facetune. I used to NEVER edit my pictures in any way, then it started with the ability to whiten my teeth and make my hair blonder, then it was pushing in my waist a little bit at a time, then my legs, then my arms, then editing my nose and face. One day I looked at my Instagram profile and my Tinder profile and I thought, you don't actually look like the person in these photos."

The omnipresence of porn culture can make these body anxieties worse. Nowadays, the easy availability of pornography has fueled a pernicious rise of genital anxiety. Porn, it turns out, makes a lot of people feel bad about their bodies and, more specifically, about their genitals. Pornland inculcates the message that your genitals should look like those of a porn star: big and perfect porno penis capable of holding an endless erection for a guy, vulva shaved and trim like a Barbie clamshell for a gal. Young people can worry they look weird or lacking "down there." This genital anxiety, for girls, is related to shaming and ignorance around menstruation. Both

phenomena are addressed today with growing movements of period positivity and genital positivity.

> "I think that porn is one of the main sources of genital anxiety for men and women. In porn, most vulvas or penises look the same and become the unreachable norm. Men can be shamed about the length or shape of their penis, while women feel shame about the size or shape of their vulva and vagina. From the perspective of a male, I often felt like I didn't look 'man enough.'"

Social media can, again, be part of both the problem and the solution. Crowdsourced websites help with self-conscious insecurity about intimate body parts. Innovative web projects normalize diversity by featuring nonsexualized photo galleries of breasts and vulvas, sent in by the women themselves. For example, 007b.com (the quirky name is pronounced "double-oh-seven-B," as in James Bond intelligence work, but using commonsense intelligence in regard to breasts) is devoted to spreading knowledge and helping women feel better about their breasts. The site's main message? "Sizes and shapes vary enormously. So don't worry, ladies!" Its gallery of photos demonstrates the huge range among breasts, areolas, and nipples. It reveals how very common is sagging and asymmetry of the breasts. It de-fetishizes the breast as a sexual organ by teaching about the natural function of breastfeeding. Similarly, Gynodiversity.com showcases photos of "real-life lady parts" that women submit of their vulvas: "Marvel, compare, and it will become clear that

Intactivism is a movement of education and activism against routine infant circumcision in favor of leaving the infant penis intact. Circumcision rates vary hugely around the world, with over 70 percent of penises circumcised in the US but only 11 percent in Germany. In America, anti-circumcision advocates march in Pride parades to celebrate the natural penis and work against "foreskin shaming." Organizations in this area include Intact America.

there are no 'standard' lady parts and that yours are perfectly normal too." Such educational websites empower viewers to embrace body variation as essential to the very definition of beauty instead of expending time, money, and anxiety to fit the body to an impossible and boring ideal of sameness.

> "Both men and women constantly talk about boobs to their friends. The 'sexy' standard for breasts is that they're big and the areola is small. This can cause dread and anxiety for women when their breasts don't meet these standards. I think that being able to see breasts in all shapes and sizes is great for personal anxieties."

#PeriodPositive: *Period positivity* aims to end stigma around menstruation. Check out the organization Period Positive, with their great tagline "It's about bloody time!" More and more, we're seeing a focus on policies around menstrual equity. In the field of international development, menstrual health management identifies *period poverty* as a barrier to girls' education and facilitates affordable access to menstrual products as a key aspect of gender equity and empowerment.

Artists play an important role in this work as well. The British artist Jamie McCartney crafted a brilliant twenty-six-feet-long exhibit cheekily entitled *The Great Wall of Vagina* that consists of casts of four hundred women's genitals (vulvas, really, but the clever punning on the Great Wall of China wouldn't work then). McCartney wanted to help people feel good about their bodies and accept them in all their natural glory (he produces art about male genitals and penises too). His website features the tagline "Changing female body image through art" and proclaims that "freedom from genital anxiety is the goal." Part of his motivation was this worrisome rise in poor body self-image, coupled with rising rates of labiaplasty surgery. This cosmetic procedure cuts off "excess" labia minora tissue in order to produce a more streamlined and symmetrical-looking vulva; the American Society of Aesthetic Plastic Surgeons reports a 217 percent increase from 2012 to 2017 in requests for these labiaplasty procedures.

Women, I suspect, didn't used to worry about these things. How would a gal even know her labia were larger than average, before Pornland made the shorn pudenda de rigueur? Many women, in fact, have inner labia longer than their outer labia majora. That's *normal*. So is asymmetry of the genitals, for both women and men. Perfect symmetry is rare. Pretty much everyone has labia that are a little lopsided or a penis and scrotum that hang either left or right. All normal, normal, normal. *The Great Wall of Vagina* and other intimate body art that McCartney has made of male genitals employ provocative visual means to highlight a simple and even demure point: diversity is the norm, all bodies are good bodies, no need to fetishize a particular type.

"Labiaplasty was a huge issue when I first became sexually active. I thought my vagina didn't 'look normal' and I even went as far as to go to a gynecologist two hours away from my hometown to get a consultation for a labiaplasty. Now, I'm so thankful that she wouldn't perform the procedure on me. I was heartbroken though. It took me a long time to feel comfortable enough with my body to become sexually active, and since then not one partner has said anything, insulted me, or spread rumors about me like I was so terrified would happen when I was sixteen!" #BodyAcceptance

"I started to think about how seeing pornographic content at a young age contributed to things like my body insecurity as an adolescent; I thought all women's naked bodies were meant to look like the perfectly manicured and proportioned ones in the sex industry. So, maybe it would have benefited me to have an adult remind me that those scenarios are not real life and are not what should be expected of you."

While I support people's right to engage in body modification and I get that many of these procedures are an empowering form of personal self-expression, let me confess that the rise of labiaplasty is a line in the sand for me. No woman should feel she needs surgery to create a Barbie-doll clamshell vulva, maintained with a monthly Brazilian, full monty wax job, just to achieve that Pornland look. All I can think is *Ouch*. Surely our genitals, among all the body parts, should most obviously be about feeling good and should not be subject to pain- and shame-inducing regimens based on how they look. Rock your gorgeous big-ass labia and your full-bush vulva, sister. Rock your stubby, side-waving penis, with or without its foreskin, brother. None of these issues affect our ability to be a great lover who gives and receives pleasure. Let no one shame us.

"I learned from a young age that body hair is gross, especially 'down there.' It is as if we as women were trained to be uncomfortable with how our body looks in its natural state. Instead, we are expected to alter it to fit the societal standard that many have come to expect. Shame and sex should not be intertwined in any way. A woman should not have to prepare herself for a sexual encounter out of fear that she will be seen as 'gross' and then have to leave without being completely fulfilled."

"There is way too much shame and secrecy around what a 'normal' vulva is supposed to look like. This used to be a big anxiety of mine. A lot of women are insecure about the way their vaginas look or feel. There is a large pressure on women to always be groomed and neat and have the 'perfect vagina' that is always ready for business. The truth is, having a different shape or size compared to someone else does not mean that yours is wrong; it simply means it is different. I hope women realize that we are all unique and that is not a bad thing."

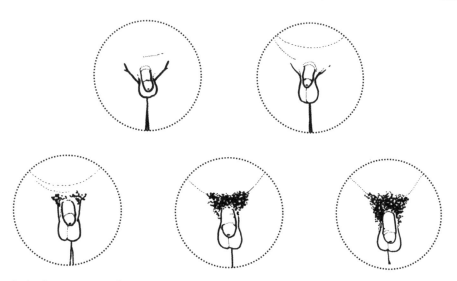

In body positivity, diversity is the norm—as it is with genitals too!

The challenge for body positivity is to repeatedly center its message: It's not about looking good. It's about feeling good. Even as the movement uses the internet's visual platforms to spread its philosophy of self-acceptance and holistic health, body positivity needs to continuously resist and subvert these platforms' pressures for optic performance. The problem is partly one of the deep cultural bias toward the beautiful that feeds into this visual pressure. A long-standing prejudice equates the physically attractive with the morally good. You see it in fairy tales, where good characters are beautiful and bad ones are ugly. The princess heroine is lovely to look at, and the wicked witch is hideous, old, and wrinkled. In language, the word *fair* carries this same double meaning, as in "The rules of the game are fair" and also "That person is very fair of face." The moral and the good-looking are closely intertwined in this cultural bias.

"People always say to not care what people think of you because you are the only person living your life, but I think most people have a desire to be desired. Women are being told to love our bodies and own them, but what do we do when that comes at the expense of finding love?"

There are implications here for issues related to penis circumcision such as female genital cutting or mutilation (see also chapter 21) and surgeries on the genitals of babies born with intersex conditions of differences in sex development. Advocates against these procedures use umbrella terms such as *genital autonomy* and *genital integrity*. These procedures raise complex issues of consent, medical justification, parenting responsibilities, religious and cultural context, and human rights. For one such discussion of intersex issues, see the United Nations awareness campaign Free and Equal. See also the organization Genital Autonomy America.

And yet, as everyone knows, the person judged most beautiful by society is by no means the nicest. Part of what body positivity does is simply point out this truth. Being beautiful is not all it's cracked up to be, and it takes a whole lot of work and fuss, to boot. This truth, however, doesn't cancel out the powerful cultural messaging around beauty. It just makes that messaging even more complex, particularly for women who are subject to it more so than men. In this changing time, women are told the body acceptance movement now frees them to #LoveYourCurves and own your #BellyJelly, but those other cultural scripts still harangue women to look sexy and young and yet simultaneously shame and dismiss them if their skirt is too short or their makeup too much. These impossible double and triple binds exert intense pressure: be hot but pure, women are told—and make it look effortless, all at the same time, to show you're enlightened enough to see through the shallowness of the beauty trap.

"Women no longer accept that they are not beautiful in their own skin."

What if #LoveYourBody and "Inhabit your body with joy!" don't work for you as slogans to live by? What if the insistence "All bodies are beautiful!" just feels like the imposition of a new cultural script? Yes, self-acceptance is a fine goal and inhabiting your body with joy an equally fine plan, but joy is a high bar. Maybe too high a bar for an average day. Maybe even feeling good in your body is too high a bar. Maybe you don't give a damn about beauty or "looking good" in any form. We need to ensure that body positivity doesn't become yet another source of beratement, yet more pressure to perform according to script.

> "I believe the message should not be that everyone is equally beautiful, but that beauty just does not matter. What you look like has no bearing on who you are as an individual."

To address these concerns, the concept of *body neutrality* is sometimes employed, as opposed to that of body positivity. The slogan "All bodies are good" works better than "All bodies are beautiful" as a way to de-emphasize that toxic cult of beauty. Advocating a more neutral attitude toward the body may work better for people for whom the body is not a source of joy. Some people reject the beauty game and "confidence culture" as rigged against them from the start.

Some people live with chronic pain. Some have progressive and degenerative health conditions. Some legitimately feel betrayed by their body. It can be very hard to feel positive about your body or to inhabit it with joy if that body has been harmed by an abuser or systematically shamed by society. Trauma is tragically ubiquitous. For people who are survivors of abuse and violence, their body may always be for them that traumatic site of suffering. A focus on their body may trigger feelings of powerlessness and humiliation.

> "I have heard so many times that us girls deserve what we get by the way we dress. We don't deserve to get raped because we show off some cleavage or our stomach. That's not how it should be."

So, what does body positivity look like for survivors of sexual assault and of more subtle forms of sexual wrongdoing and slut-shaming? What does it look like for people who've been fat-shamed all their lives? Disabled people who've been made to feel they should hide their bodies out of public sight? People of color whose dark skin has been a site of stigma and hate? People who've been told in a million and one subtle and not-so-subtle ways that their body doesn't fit the ideal and never will? People whose self-confidence has been battered along with their physical selves?

> "My partner has a history of traumatic emotional and sexual abuse with an ex-boyfriend and it's incredibly emotional for her. She has diagnosed PTSD and occasionally has involuntary body spasms while we're intimate."

The messages of body positivity, in such cases, can make you feel at fault, like a failure, if you aren't confident enough or joyous enough to love your body and sashay it down the road no matter your love handles or stretch marks, your soft belly, your wrinkles and sags, your ebony skin, your disabled limbs, your body as a site of remembered trauma. It's easy to say, "All bodies are beautiful," but that ease may be the privilege of the person whose body has not borne the scorn of society.

> "Although I agree with the general message of body positivity and loving the skin you are in, I believe that it still lacks diverse representation. I have a physical disability, and the relationship between disability and body image is often overlooked. Having a physical disability often means that your body changes against your will and it is often out of your control. This combines with the reality that your body is seen as 'less than' in society is very harmful to body image."

The body positive movement is not here to re-traumatize anyone, nor to impose any new burden. The movement needs to make room for some people's sense that their body is *not* good, not beautiful, harmed and not recovered, maybe not as good as it used to be, maybe not good enough. If you don't feel like loving your body with a vengeance, that's okay too. There is no victim-blaming in body positivity. Flaunt your belly jelly or not, as you wish. It's totally your choice. Self-esteem, self-acceptance, and embracing your body will look different for different people. Not everyone has to strip down on the beach to prove they are "woke" enough, with the requisite degree of self-acceptance, to be a bo-po warrior.

To tweak the message: love thyself and practice self-care in whatever form is appropriate for you, as we work together in our flawed world toward a future of body justice and equity for all.

Chapter 13

Sex is not only for the young and beautiful

One powerful way to ensure body positivity doesn't fall short of its potential is to highlight not just the diversity of all bodies but also their sexual citizenship. The movement maintains its impact—its force of transgressive provocation and resistance to banal or too-easy messaging—through this full-throated insistence: sex is not only for the young and the beautiful. Not only *All bodies are good bodies*, but *All bodies are sexy bodies*, as sexy as they care to be.

Many companies in the industries of fashion retail and personal grooming products have embraced body positivity along exactly this message. Marketing and advertising campaigns are increasingly built around it, with prideful portraits of diverse body types all presented as sexy and gorgeous. Dove soap was an early adopter, with the award-winning "Dove Campaign for Real Beauty" that started in 2004. Their innovative ads showcased women who were nonprofessional models in order to celebrate "real" and diverse bodies, including women of size and older women, and to widen the definition of beauty beyond narrow stereotypes. Aerie, the lingerie brand of clothing retailer American Eagle, continued this conversation about positive body image under #AerieReal with a refusal to Photoshop its models and taglines such as "We think the real you is sexy." Most recently, Aerie ran a campaign of even more radical body positivity, featuring women who modeled bras and underwear while in their wheelchair or showing their insulin pumps or ostomy bags. Such a messaging strategy grabs media and consumer attention; it feels strong, brave, and exactly of the moment.

"Rihanna has become a huge front runner for body acceptance with her Savage X Fenty lingerie line. Sexy Clothes for ALL SHAPES!!"

Attention grabbing also are campaigns that switch the gender messaging onto men: body-inclusive campaigns showcasing authentic diversity of male bodies. Traditional notions of masculinity are very much tied into norms of a muscled physique. In deliberate opposition to such notions, various brands of men's underwear—Hanes, Jockey, the European men's clothing brand Dressman, the British label Surge—have all run innovative male body-positive ad campaigns. Their marketing includes male models who are older, trans, disabled, and fat, in order to highlight a wide range of body types and to make the point that there's more than one way to embody masculinity.

"From the time I can remember, my sisters and I would watch the Victoria's Secret Fashion Show and be so in awe of them because they are all truly the unrealistic beauty standard for women, but you never saw bigger women on the runway with them. Skinny was literally everywhere, so we grew up thinking that's the goal and that's what men love and find attractive. If we hadn't seen all of those images, maybe it would've been different."

The body positive trend has become so pronounced that brands who resist it seem out of step with the times—to the detriment of the brand's image and the company's bottom line. The decline of the iconic lingerie behemoth Victoria's Secret stands as a prime example. After years of dominating its market and the frenzied media hype around its annual fashion show featuring skinny supermodels sporting angels' wings, Victoria's Secret fortunes plummeted. The former retail leader now feels tired and tone-deaf, stuck with their hypersexualized and unattainable "angelic" ideal (although they have attempted their own body-positive rebrand, replacing their Angels with "The VS Collective"), while competitors gain ground with fresh body-inclusive messaging. Women's plus-sized clothing retailer Lane Bryant even launched a defiant send-up against Victoria's Secret under the sassy tagline "I'm No Angel."

It is, however, this very success of body positivity that causes concern. Once the movement becomes commercialized—adopted as a CSR (corporate social responsibility) campaign of socially conscious cause marketing, in the business-school lingo—it opens itself to accusations of compromise and selling out. Are brands jumping on the body-positive bandwagon merely for the optics of the activism and without deep commitment? It can't just be about companies wanting to cash in on the wave by featuring a little pudge or some lighter-skinned people of color in their ads. As body positivity achieves mainstream cultural impact—as its message is, yes, inevitably monetized—it needs to stay focused on its core commitment to real diversity of representation for the fullest range of body types in advertising, TV and film, social media content, fashion, and all the body-based industries. A shallow performative activism is not enough.

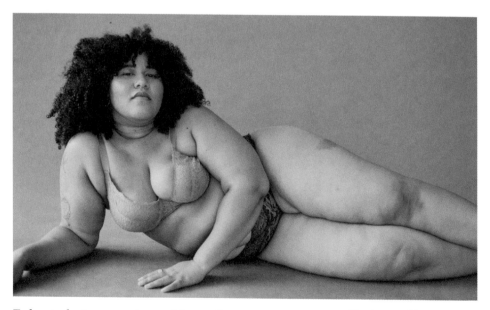

Today, inclusive campaigns celebrate diverse representations of bodies and beauty.

The point highlights a risk in the body acceptance movement: the re-imposition of an ideal in the definition of what counts as sexy and attractive. The risk is that as body positivity grows, it becomes co-opted and slides back into a shame-driven body mandate. The issue of women's body weight—that perennial bugaboo—provides an example of this risk. Today, due to the success of body acceptance, it's become okay for a woman to be *thick*. It might even be better to be thick. Thick is *sexy*. But a couple of problems arise. Body positivity betrays its mission of social justice if its critique against fat-shaming spawns a reverse backlash of skinny-shaming. Slurs against fat people aren't defeated by replacing them with slurs against "skinny bitches," as in Meghan Trainor's 2014 pro-booty pop megahit "All About That Bass." (Although she did add the line "No, I'm just playing.")

A related problem is that only a certain type of thick flies: the desired shape is curvy, with a busty chest, indented waist, and flat stomach, broadening out to that requisite round ass and hips. Maybe fat but not too fat. Thick but still hourglass. The belly can jiggle, but it shouldn't *hang*. But what if you don't want to cinch in your waist and hoist up your boobs into buxom cleavage? Not so Insta-worthy now.

"I, as an African American woman, have heard countless Black men term women as thick that simply had a larger backside. I, for one, have been coined 'too skinny' and not 'thick,' which made me become very self-conscious and insecure. Besides being told in school I was not meeting the thick quota, I would have to listen to songs that stressed how the perfect women should look. Also, we live in a society where celebrities attempt to achieve this idea of a perfect figure and invest heavily in plastic surgery and other cosmetics fixes. We began to think that we must work out every day or go on intense celebrity diets. It should never be normalized for people of any size to feel they may never find love because of their image. People are beautiful in any image they choose."

There's a common root to both these problems: authentic body positivity does not involve pressure toward the latest trend in the social construction of beauty standards, whether it be thinness or thickness. The movement is not about making money off a new body ideal but about authentic diversity of representation in which the autonomy and sexuality of all bodies are respected. It's about saying there's more than one right way to embody or express gender identity and sexuality. There will be no revolution if visual culture gets taken over yet again by the curvy-but-slim-and-pale-groomed beauty norms that the movement set out to upend.

> "How do we as a society make the darker-skinned women feel more accepted and loved, the same way we make the lighter-skinned women get all the praise and respect? It's no question that white women have co-opted the body positive movement. There should be more representation of all skin types and body types in the ads and movies. We want to make everyone feel accepted, but we as a society are doing the exact opposite. It's important to stick together and not to knock each other down, no matter the skin color, the career choice, or the size of our bodies."

An emphasis on *sexual citizenship* helps body positivity maintain its inclusive radical heart. All bodies have the right to sexual citizenship. Everyone has the right to be recognized as a sexual being with sexual agency, their body associated with sexuality and their desire honored. Everyone has the right to experience their own body's sexual pleasure and to share consensual pleasure with others. The point returns us to the discussion of asexuality from chapter 9. In a visual culture obsessed with youth and beauty, certain demographics of people are consistently and falsely presumed to be asexual and their sexuality is denied. Society's sexual scripts, traditionally skewed to the young and the beautiful or the male and the powerful, unfairly restrict recognition of full sexual citizenship to that narrow range of people. Others get desexualized.

> "Every day, I am attacked by my pictures and videos of fit and sexy women reminding me that I am not one of them. I use a wheelchair. I do not see sexy pictures of women who look like me on Facebook or on a cover of a magazine. For a long time, I thought my body was not sexy, and no one would ever see me as a sexual person. I have learned to love my body and to embrace it, but my self-confidence is still lacking and so is the body diversities in magazines and social media."

Older people, disabled people, and fat people are all often treated as if they are devoid of sexuality—or as if they should be. Their entire demographic is dismissed as unsexy or as existing outside the realm of the sexual. They become invisible. Their sexual autonomy is negated and their desire ridiculed as gross, laughable, or inappropriate. Body positivity fights against this presumed asexuality of the body deemed ugly, of the nerdy geek body, of the fatter body, the elderly body, the disabled body. Even the female body is denied its full sexuality to the extent that women are encouraged to be sexy but not sexual. Women are expected to exude sex appeal and to pleasure men, but a woman who desires and demands sex for her own satisfaction violates social norms and is easily demonized as monstrous. Body positivity fights against *all* these stereotypes of who is and isn't worthy of being recognized in their own right as a full, active sexual agent.

> "I have a chronic disease that is an invisible illness. I'm not quite sure why people think that individuals with disabilities aren't going to be sexually active. They are just as much human as anyone else; their disability doesn't define them. Humans want to have sex and just because you have a disability or chronic disease doesn't mean that will change. I'm very lucky to have a boyfriend who is caring and all-around amazing. Sex for me has been a learning experience because my body can't always move and do things that I want, but my boyfriend is so understanding and wants to do whatever is most comfortable for me."

In the new gender and sexual revolution, body positivity widens the category of the sexy. It widens the right of sexual citizenship and autonomy. By promoting inclusion, the body acceptance movement accords visibility and respect. It celebrates, without mockery or condescension, the full sexual humanity of us all.

Where does this moment of cultural change take us next? By broadening these scripts about the good and sexy body and how to embody gender, the Manisexto proclaims the end of body shaming and gender bullying. The ground is cleared for the next shift in how we talk about gender and sexuality: the #MeToo movement. Previously, toxic gender scripts muddied consent and contributed to rape. But today, new conversations have people discussing the foundations of good sex in unprecedented ways.

Time for point 4: the bedrock importance of consent.

Manisexto #4

CONSENT

Full Consent Is Fundamental to All Sexual Activity

Chapter 14

THE ROLE OF CONSENT IN GOOD SEX

The sex talk of the moment? It's all about *consent*.

Through the impact of the #MeToo movement, consent has become the most salient lesson about sex: you have to get a "yes" before you can get intimate. What's emerged is a torrent of shared stories about how sexual harassment or assault has happened to "me too" and a growing cultural consensus that nonconsensual sexual encounters are not to be tolerated. It's one of the most significant and hopeful developments to emerge from the new gender and sexual revolution.

"We are at a very exciting time in our history. There are a lot of important issues being discussed right now. Because of movements such as #MeToo and Black Lives Matter, we are seeing systemic problems getting addressed. We are now talking about sexual assault and holding offenders accountable. We are talking about toxic masculinity and the actions needed to shift it. There is a real hunger in this world to move forward and do better."

Cases of violent rape—the archetypal "stranger with a knife in a dark alley" sort of rape—are easy enough to identify and condemn (not that the prosecution of such rapists and the defense of sexual justice has ever been the legal system's highest priority). Increasingly, however, a broad public conversation condemns less obvious but no less harmful instances of misconduct. Not all sexual assaults involve physical violence. Resilient victims and survivors are telling their stories not only of stranger rape but also of acquaintance rape, abuse in work situations, coercion in dating relationships, and exploitation of youth by trusted adults. We're becoming much better at recognizing the variety of forms of sexual wrongdoing, speaking out against these behaviors, punishing the perpetrators, and supporting the survivors.

When the "MeToo" hashtag went viral in October 2017—on Facebook, *4.7 million people* used the hashtag within twenty-four hours—it prompted a national and international wave of activism. Suddenly, people were talking like never before about sexual harassment in the media and entertainment industries, in politics and the workplace. As a movement of empowerment and solidarity, #MeToo has raised awareness about how incredibly widespread the problem of sexual misconduct is. The flood of stories about unwanted sexual advances, while so disheartening and enraging, inspire

#MeToo is a movement of empowerment and solidarity.

with their moral courage. #MeToo has lessened stigma about speaking up to share one's story as a survivor of abuse. By breaking the silence, the movement shows people they aren't alone.

When the "MeToo" hashtag went viral in October 2017, 4.7 million people used it on Facebook within twenty-four hours.

Although the #MeToo movement brought consent front and center into an ongoing discussion, even before the hashtag blew up on social media, consent talk had already taken hold in the realm of higher education. Over the past decade, American colleges and universities have paid increasing attention to sexual and gender justice. This new focus relates to rising reports of campus sexual assault (the rise is almost certainly in the incidence of re-porting—which is a *good* thing—and not in the actual incidence of assault). In 2011, the US Department of Educa-tion issued guidelines to clarify that the gender equity law called Title IX ap-plied to sexual violence at institutions of higher education. Title IX creates an ob-ligation—one that is regulatory but also ethical and ultimately financial because of the threat of fines and lawsuits—for schools to maintain gender equality not only in their sports programming but also in protecting their students from rape and sexual harassment.

> "48% of Female Undergrads at Duke Say They Were Sexually Assaulted While Enrolled"—headline of article in the *Chronicle of Higher Education*, February 22, 2019. The article reports that "the most common time for undergraduate women to be assaulted was during September of their freshman year," a time period that's come to be called the "Red Zone."

"Being in college, I know a great amount of girls who have been raped."

The press and the popular culture became consumed by stories of sex-ual assault on college campuses. One infamous example was 2015's Brock

In 2014, the Obama-Biden White House launched the national organization It's On Us to "combat campus sexual assault by engaging all students, including young men." It's now the nation's largest grassroots program dedicated to preventing college sexual violence and supporting survivors.

Turner case at Stanford University, when Turner, a nineteen-year-old student athlete, was convicted of sexually assaulting Chanel Miller, whose powerful victim impact statement led to her award-winning memoir *Know My Name* and helped spur a national conversation about honoring rape survivors. This heightened awareness forced schools to respond and to confront the prevalence of acquaintance rape amid campus hookup culture. Universities came up with enhanced procedures to deal with incidents of sexual assault and with programs to teach students about bystander intervention, alcohol awareness, and—above all—consent.

"I am a twenty-year-old woman college student and I constantly hear stories about my friends or friends of friends who were assaulted by somebody else at a bar or a party. I, myself, can even admit that I too have been sexually assaulted before, and it is one of the hardest things to admit to yourself and believe. One of my close friends was sexually assaulted badly, and it ended up changing her ENTIRE college experience and life. She went from a presidential scholar to almost failing out."

In tandem with #MeToo, a national movement of education and prevention has arisen on campuses around sexual misconduct. More than ever before, schools are affirming values of sexual justice: a commitment to creating a positive climate for healthy sexuality within the campus community. Such a commitment embraces, on the one hand, inclusion and equity for the diversity of sexual orientation and gender identity and, on the other hand, the requirement of full consent as foundational for any sexual activity. The cynical reading is that schools pay lip service to these values of sexual justice while simultaneously allowing the conditions for sexual misconduct and homophobic toxic masculinity to thrive, by tacitly condoning an alcohol-soaked party scene fueled by big-money college sports and a Greek system of white-privilege fraternities and sororities. The student comments in this chapter and the next illustrate these conflicting messages within higher education.

While women suffer higher rates of sexual assault, an important new understanding coming to light because of #MeToo is how often *males* are victims of sexual misconduct as well. Guys, in fact, suffer from an even greater cultural taboo against reporting sexual assault, such that it can be hard for them to acknowledge they've been assaulted. The gender script for masculinity says they're supposed to be tough and strong and always up for sex, so how can a "real man" be raped or harassed? But the new realization is that sexual assault can happen to anyone. Not just children and not just women. The victims of sexual violence are people of all genders, all sexual orientations, all backgrounds.

"I was sexually assaulted last summer. I struggled with thinking about it and for months completely pushed it out of my brain. I felt so alone and isolated. I think it's ironic that, at least in my social circles, we always believe women when they come forward. Yet in my same friend group, when I tried to talk about my assault the first response was "Chill out, dude, maybe they just thought you're sexy"—as if that was anywhere near the response we would've given a girl who experienced the same thing. The pain of being a male sexual assault victim is made so much worse by no one understanding."

Through these realms of higher education, the legal system, the court of public opinion, and the world of social media and the Twittersphere, society is granting more space for people to bravely come forward and report their experiences of unwanted intimacy. The result is a game-changing and culture-wide reckoning with sexual misconduct. From the #MeToo survivor stories, we're gaining a detailed picture about the conditions that invalidate consent. We're talking, finally, about what it means to take consent seriously.

A major recent book about the problem of sexual assault in higher education is ***Sexual Citizens: A Landmark Study of Sex, Power, and Assault on Campus*** (2020). Based on research conducted at Columbia University in New York City through the Sexual Health Initiative to Foster Transformation (SHIFT) by book authors Professors Jennifer Hirsch and Shamus Khan, ***Sexual Citizens*** aims to understand how the college experience leads to sexual assault for almost one in three women and one in six men and how to change the social roots of this campus phenomenon to effect lasting change.

All this conversation leads to lessons about sexual justice that are dead simple and yet surprisingly complicated. What's simple is the core message: consent is crucial. People get to choose whether they want to engage in sexual activity. Others need to respect a person's choice to not participate. Everyone needs to ask first for consent and to listen for an answer. No one should be made to engage in any sort of sexual activity against their will. That includes no sexual bullying, no groping, no catcalling on the streets, no workplace harassment, and certainly no sexual contact with minors.

Sex requires adult partners' clear agreement. Such consent is the sturdy bedrock to good sex.

"All people deserve ownership of their bodies."

And yet, the message is not so simple. And neither is it enough. The complexity arises with the very definition of consent. Real consent—informed, meaningful consent—is not just an eye-rolling *Whatever*. It's not a huffy *Oh, all right!* It's not a hesitant *Okay, I guess?* And while full consent is required for any sexual activity, even the fullest of consent doesn't guarantee good sex. You can consent and still have bad sex: disconnected from your feelings of desire, lacking in real agency, resulting in unequal pleasure and an orgasm gap. Put another way, consent is fundamental, but it's not everything. What it does give us is a place to begin.

So, what does consent in good sex look like? And—most importantly—how do we get there?

Chapter 15

WHAT CONSENT IS (GOOD COMMUNICATION) AND IS NOT (GREEN EGGS AND HAM OR A BLANKET)

Let's start with green eggs and ham, where the lesson from the dating world and hookup scene is that nobody is entitled to sex. And nobody owes anyone else an orgasm.

Sex—and sexual consent—is not green eggs and ham. Dr. Seuss's iconic children's book *Green Eggs and Ham* makes the point that sometimes you need to try something in order to know if you like it or not. Sometimes you think you really do not want to eat green eggs and ham, but someone else is convinced they know better and will urge you, coax you, and even stalk you into trying their dish—"Would you? Could you? In a car? Eat them! Eat them! Here they are!"—until you give up and give in, out of exasperation, because their persistence leaves you with no other choice.

This message about consent applies to a wider realm than just sex. It's good advice in general. Everybody wants to have their privacy respected and to be able to set boundaries for their personal space and autonomy. And because everyone is different, it's often best to simply ask. For example, "Are you a hugger?" Not everyone is, and that's okay. Little kids are often grabbed for cuddles. That stereotype of the overbearing aunt or creepy uncle going in for the big bear hug and sloppy kiss? Not cool. Letting children know the choice is theirs is a great way to teach them about their right to control their body. These guidelines apply in many realms: before serving someone food or drink or giving a particular gift or event experience, ask if the person would be interested in such. Before taking photos of someone or posting them on social media. Before tickling a child. Check in first to see if *any* of that works for the person. They may have an allergy or food sensitivity, a religious prohibition, a chronic illness, a personal dislike. Any number of reasons may create preferences that are easily inquired about and taken into account instead of steamrolled over. Bottom line? Respect people's choices and don't make assumptions.

There may be a valid point here for kids, who are often fussy eaters. *Try that broccoli, little one—you might like it.* Children, with their developing taste buds, need exposure to a new flavor multiple times before they learn to like it. Parents have a right, perhaps even an obligation, to cajole their offspring into trying different foods.

Sex, it must be said very clearly, is not like learning to eat your vegetables. No insistence, hounding, wheedling, pleading, deal-making. I hear from my students, especially the women but across all gender identities, that such does happen, all the time, in matters of sex. "How about just a blow job? Maybe a hand job?" Or, "Don't you think I'm pretty? Can't you get it up?" The students call these situations a "bad hookup" or "gray-area" consent or "rape-y" sex or just outright rape. The scenarios vary in the extent to which they invalidate consent and meet the legal definition for sexual assault. But while what transpires might not be violent rape, it's certainly not good sex.

"Giving a guy oral sex to get out of a situation? I have resorted to that more times than I should. I think it's a sad reality that girls feel they have to do at least *something* for the guy instead of speaking up and saying they would like to leave, without worrying if the guy will think or speak negatively of her."

Here, then, is a key insight of our present moment of #MeToo. When people treat sex in this green-eggs-and-ham fashion—when someone pressures another into agreement—the result is a lot of sex where the consent is murky at best. The Manisexto's message on this point is that consent needs to be freely given, without coercion. If the consent is coerced, it doesn't count. What this means is *No means no* the first time. Not, *Convince me*. Not, *Maybe*. Nobody likes to be pressured. It's wrong to bully or badger or shame someone into sex. Your own honor and respect mean that you take the first no as your answer and move on. I'm referring to respect for the rights of others but to self-respect as well. You are special, worthy—we all are. If you're going to have sex with someone, they should really want you. And you should really want them. Pulsing mutual desire: hold out for that. When such desire blooms, ascertain if it's shared. If not, back off. You and your partner both deserve it. There will be other times, other partners.

"As someone who occasionally dabbles in hookup culture, I can certainly say the big problem that arises is a lack of communication. I learned that before anything happens, just laying groundwork, boundaries, expectations, likes, and dislikes all significantly improved the encounters I was having."

Alcohol also interferes with a person's ability to give informed consent. Particularly in hookup culture and the college party scene, alcohol is one of the major ways that consent can get murky, fast. It's obvious that physical force or threat invalidates consent; if there's a gun to your head or a suffocating hand around your throat, any "agreement" you give is null and void. It should be equally obvious that incapacitation invalidates consent, although given the number of cases where this scenario comes up, the point bears repeating—loudly. People who are drunk or high, intoxicated through alcohol or drugs, do not have the capacity to consent to sex. You must be sufficiently sober, in your right mind, able to know what you're doing and to evaluate the consequences, in order to grant informed consent and to participate in sex. Anyone who takes advantage of an incapacitated person to have sex with them is committing a sexual assault.

> "Personally, I have heard the story of a friend who got very drunk at a party one night. He went to go lay down on his bed to sleep off the alcohol because he could barely move. A girl he knew came into his room, saw him lying there, pulled down the incoherent boy's pants, and proceeded to have sex with him. This girl sexually assaulted the drunk boy."

> "I have a friend who was sexually assaulted her freshman year of college by a guy who decided her being unconscious and drunk somehow equated to consent."

Consent is likewise invalidated or hollowed out if a big power differential creates imbalance in a relationship and opens up the possibility of exploitation. Such interactions are sometimes referred to as "vertical relationships": situations marked by a hierarchy, where one person has significant authority or duty of care over another. Think doctor and patient, teacher and student, minister/priest and congregant, guard and prisoner, supervisor and intern, employer and employee. Romances along these lines used to be more socially accepted: the boss dating the secretary or the professor going out with the graduate student. Now, such pairings can get you fired. They are explicitly banned at my university, as at many schools. High-profile examples from the business world include McDonald's ousting its CEO Steve Easterbrook in 2019 and CNN president Jeff Zucker resigning in 2022, both for carrying out a relationship with an employee against company policy. "Grooming" is a predatory example of a vertical relationship, when a trusted adult befriends a vulnerable youth, winning their confidence with gifts and flattering attention before turning the relationship into a sexual one; in more extreme cases, it becomes procurement and sex trafficking.

None of this is to say there must be absolute equality of social and economic power between people for a romantic or sexual relationship to be ethical. Such a demand would be artificial and impossible to judge. Difference is, of course, often intriguing, exciting, sexy. As the saying goes, opposites attract. But vertical relationships create the impression of favoritism within an organization, are fraught with potential for abuse of power, and leave the person with less power vulnerable to retaliation if the relationship goes sour. When one person has the ability to control some significant aspect of another's

> Laws vary from state to state; here's a summary from the criminal code of my home state of Alabama about sexual offenses and consent:
>
> Under Alabama law, sexual assault is defined as sexual intercourse or anal or oral sex (including even slight penetration with a body part or an object), if the other person does not or cannot consent, or is deceived. Consent to sexual activity cannot be given by persons who are:
>
> • physically forced or threatened with use of force (whether express or implied)
> • temporarily incapable of appraising or controlling their conduct due to the influence of a narcotic, anesthetic, or intoxicating substance
> • unconscious, asleep, or otherwise physically limited or unable to communicate
> • unable to understand the nature of the conduct due to a mental or developmental disease or disability
> • underage (generally, the age of consent is 16 years old).

life—their salary, career advancement, academic progress, spiritual direction, health care, and so on—consent is compromised and can't be granted as freely as in a more egalitarian relationship.

One last qualification: consent is not a blanket. A one-time yes does not cover everything, forever. Meaningful consent happens throughout a sexual encounter and over the entire course of a relationship. Agreeing to a date does not imply any agreement to physical intimacy. Agreeing to make out isn't agreeing to a blow job. Agreeing to oral sex isn't agreeing to penetrative sex. Agreeing to marriage doesn't entail an open-ended agreement to sex at any time (although, before the gains of the twentieth century's second-wave feminist movement, marital rape was generally considered legal). And whatever someone *does* agree to, remember they can withdraw their consent at any time; people always have the right to change their minds during an encounter.

> "Consent is not a forever ownership given to take sex whenever they want. There have been so many stories about possessive boyfriends or husbands who feel they are 'owed sex.' I've heard friends talk about how they have to have sex and don't want to and I'm always like, 'No, if you don't feel like it, you don't have to, ever.' It makes me upset and angry."

If you treat consent like a blanket, you risk assuming that your partner has agreed to a lot more than they actually have. That's why consent needs to be ongoing, why open communication needs to continue throughout sex. And if the need to obtain clear consent before initiating sexual activity sounds too legalistic and unsexy, it's not. Just use your words! Keep talking: "What are you up for?" "What feels good to you?" "Would you like to . . .?"

> "It is important to engage in a conversation not just of consent, but also preferences. The conversation of consent shouldn't just end with *yes* but should also include *What are you into?*—to normalize exploring, learning, and creating an experience. We're so scared we're going to be bad at sex and that our reputation or relationships will suffer because of poor performance. How do we normalize 'sexploration' and get over the awkwardness of trying something new?"

This ongoing good consent is affirmative: not simply the absence of a no, but the presence of a yes. Just because someone's not yelling stop or trying to leave the room does not mean they're giving you the go-ahead. The best consent is nonambiguous verbal agreement that uses clearly articulated and enthusiastic language. It's full-throated, not half-hearted. Don't rely solely on body language for this go-ahead, as gestures can easily be misinterpreted, especially in the drunken or lusty heat of the moment (does that hand on the chest mean *back off* or *come closer*?). It is important, however, to be attentive to body language that is hesitant or fearful, to someone who becomes quiet or passive or nonresponsive during an intimate encounter. #MeToo has taught us much about fear paralysis, the "freeze response" that immobilizes a person who feels threatened, and that can be as common as the better-known "fight or flight." Real consent is active, not passive; it involves an enthused and engaged response.

"About enthusiastic consent: I have been on the other end of this, and it is haunting. Wondering afterwards, *Did the person really want that?* If the consent is not wholly convincing and committed, it is going to cause problems. I think looking at tomorrow instead of tonight and evaluating how people will feel the next day is a pretty safe way to go about things."

In all these problematic scenarios, note the common element: taking advantage of a situation in order to exert power over another person and to satisfy one's sexual desire. If you want to call yourself a good person, you need to agree with the statement that all sexual activity must be fully consensual. You need to be committed to that bedrock importance of consent. You and any partner should be sober enough, in your right minds, to know what you're doing, to easily articulate what you want, and to take steps to keep yourselves safe from sexually transmitted diseases and unwanted pregnancy. No one should be feeling badgered or pressured. There should be enough equality between partners that nobody's too bedazzled or intimidated to refuse the encounter.

Relationship violence (also called intimate partner violence, interpersonal violence, or domestic violence when the partners share a home) does not always involve physical abuse. The violence can be emotional, verbal, or technological in nature. Examples of emotional abuse include manipulating, belittling, using guilt or fear to control someone, isolating someone from friends or family, and causing distress through harassment or threats. Verbal abuse includes insults, the spread of rumors, and the use of humiliating slurs. Technological abuse involves cyberstalking, posting revenge porn, spying and tracking via social media, and sending repeated unwanted messages. One excellent resource and advocacy group is the Washington, DC–based National Network to End Domestic Violence. Learn more at nnedv.org.

"Instead of unspoken pressures, there should be communicated desires."

This new and deeper understanding of consent is not, in the end, at all complicated. Consent simply means everyone involved freely agrees they want to be involved. In its essence, consent is about good communication in a two-way relationship. It means your agreement about sex is clear, informed, active, enthused, continuous, free of coercion, mutually desired, and between more or less equal adult partners. It's how you know you're a good person.

"Getting clear consent is not difficult if you make a point of discussing it, and it can even be sexy!"

The new gender and sexual revolution breaks down taboos that silence survivors. It condemns all forms of non-consensual sex. The concept of consent does a lot to get us to healthy intimate relationships, but we don't get there fully without addressing in more depth a very important topic that's come up a few times now: the gender scripts.

Good sex requires that we tackle what these scripts have to say about masculinity and femininity. We need better notions of what it means to be a sexually active woman or man or gender-nonbinary person. Here, then, is another way to think about consent: girls shouldn't be forced into the role of gatekeeper nor boys into a "Man Box." Getting the gender scripts right, opening them up to new and more inclusive understandings, is a crucial part of consensual relationships.

Chapter 16

SAYING YES, SAYING NO, EXPANDING THE GENDER SCRIPTS

Let's back up a bit. Despite the prevalence of consent language and its success in advancing the sexual justice goals of the #MeToo movement, there's a problem with talking about good sex in terms of consent. As a framework for teaching moral and legal behavior, the concept is burdened with certain limitations.

The structural logic of consent is that one person proposes something and another person either consents to the proposal or declines it. One person initiates an offer, and the other responds. One asks for permission; the other answers. The notion implies that one person is an active instigator and the other has a more passive role of receiving the request, although this role does then grant them their own sphere of action—one of secondary *re*-action.

The problem is, if one person is always leading the interaction, then the two roles lack balance and full equality. From this perspective, maybe it's not consent but something more like agreement that we should be talking about. A framework of *mutual agreement* might be better than *consent* as alternative language and a more egalitarian way of ensuring that people are communicating and deciding together, on equal footing, how best to proceed. As I noted earlier when discussing the related term *consensus* in chapter 7, the root meaning of the word *consent* is, in fact, "to feel together," derived from the Latin verb *consentire*. Ironically, the imbalance between consent's two roles belies this original mutuality implied by the term.

Here is the heart of the matter: the complication with the concept of consent is how its imbalanced dynamic of initiator and respondent plays into culture's imbalanced gender roles. Consent language maintains the unequal dynamic in the traditional gender scripts. Consent is problematic to the extent that it keeps this dynamic intact. Thus, this core problem of consent discourse is the problem of the gender scripts within patriarchy. We don't get to the "feel together" / mutual agreement type of consent—to full and meaningful consent—without achieving more balanced and egalitarian gender roles.

> "The problems with gender norms can't just be acknowledged; they need to be changed. Without altering the gendered social roles, sexual assault itself will not magically disappear. We need to transform the way men think about masculinity in order to drive real societal change."

The difficulty lies in the boxed-in gender scripting itself. Scripts circulate in the culture as narratives about gender and the body, story lines about how gender is supposed to be embodied and expressed. Children learn to perform gender by internalizing these directives about how to live out— and how we are all meant to live up to—norms of manhood and womanhood. Traditionally, the scripts bifurcate gender into two boxes—the M and the F, the binary of male and female. These gender binaries are depicted as opposites that are aligned in a hierarchical fashion and that are intended to complement and complete each other through a requisite heterosexual matchup.

All this ties into older notions of the man as the breadwinner and provider and of the woman as the homemaker and nurturer. In a patriarchy, these gender scripts have written the man as dominant (competent, in control, exercising power, capable of violence) and the woman as submissive (compliant, docile, pleasing to others, the nice girl). Even with all the massive gains of feminism, changes in the workforce, and media examples of strong women, the central message of these scripts lingers on: the essential nature of masculinity is to lead and of femininity to follow. The narrative has not disappeared that he initiates and she responds.

> "I have a guy friend, more like a 'friends with benefits' situation, but we both know there's deeper feelings. I think he is just scared to take the next step, so for now I am remaining in my throne type of energy, making it clear I will never chase him and allowing him to still hold his place of being masculine and dominating. But I believe the norm of men needing to be seen as dominant and tough all of the time by bottling up feelings is only setting them up for failure. We need to change this notion of masculinity to become a thing of being confident and bold while owning your emotions, because then it can be seen as courageous and brave and people look up to you because you are owning your power from a higher vibrating state, instead of feeling forced to feed your ego to make people think you are the ultimate alpha male."

This gendered pattern holds true in the scripts of romance and sex. Think ballroom dancing: the man is supposed to lead, the woman to follow. It's the man's role to ask the woman out on the date; the man's role, still today, to propose marriage and offer the ring. In traditional heteronormative culture, the default script for sex is penis-in-vagina intercourse: it's the man's role to penetrate the woman. While this pattern of aggrandizing the male role over the female is heterosexual, it can hold even within gay communities, as proof of the extent to which the feminine has secondary social status within the logic of the gender scripts.

These gendered sexual scripts have a lot to say about how appropriate sexual conduct differs for men and women, based on another difference assumed to be inherent in the gender binary: men's and women's unequal levels of libido. A standard assumption embedded in consent discourse is that it's about a guy wanting to have sex and a woman deciding whether to do it with him or not. It's about guys asking, because, *duh*, they're the guys, the ones who are the active sexual agents; men are expected to be horny and assertive about their desire. And it's about women saying yes or no, because they're the ones presumed to be less horny and more passive in their desire, whose role is to respond to—and to satisfy—the guy's desire.

> "I am part of the LGBTQIA+ community. Having friends who are openly gay, I have noticed sometimes there is a fear of sounding or acting 'too fem' or 'being a twink' and men are quick to attack each other if those boundaries are crossed. Part of me wonders if this is because of how people continue unhealthy gender norms from their upbringing or if it is due to how gay men are portrayed in popular media and the stigma we still have associated with being gay."

> "I am angry that I have been denied crucial information, subjected to sexual assault due to my lack of knowledge, and stripped of feeling comfortable in my own body. Even with a trusting partner, my long-term boyfriend of two years, I still felt a deep sense of shame about sex. I thought there was something wrong with me. I was raised as a feminist by a strong grandmother and mother. I demand egalitarianism in most aspects of my life, but I had been cheated by society and fooled into believing that the sex that I was accustomed to was the sex that I deserved. Sexuality is extremely taboo among women, despite hookup culture and the normalization of sex. Women are groomed to be submissive and trained to think that their pleasure is dependent on their partners. Even as our society continues to become more egalitarian, sex is the one aspect of our culture that still strongly benefits men."

When these dynamics play out in heterosexual encounters, women get placed in what's called a "gatekeeper" role. Their role becomes to guard, so to speak, the gate to the vulva. Within this gender script, men are always going to be knocking on that door. That's what men are told to do, in order to live up to the code of manhood. A woman's role as gatekeeper is to restrain both his sexuality and her own. His sexuality is overdetermined by the gender script, whereas she, as the "good" woman, is cast in an almost asexual light, denied the full right of her own desire.

> "In high school, my parents found out I was sexually texting my girlfriend. They verbally attacked her, while maintaining me as a saint. It felt like such a double standard, even though we were both participating in the act, that she was deemed a whore and no good, but I was forgivable because I was a man seeking pleasure while she was a woman seeking pleasure. All teenagers going through puberty are going to be sexually frustrated, but it seems only to be acceptable for males to act on it, even though a female is going through the same thing."

So, how does a young woman learn to prioritize her own needs and desires? It's not easily done. Despite the significant gains of gender equity, the popular culture and visual media still feed the lesson that women are supposed to look attractive to men and that their power comes from granting or withholding access to sex. These messages condition girls and women to prioritize male pleasure over their own. The gender script grooms girls, just as a sexual offender does, winning her over. The script lures and seduces girls into accepting their assigned gatekeeper role with promises of the role's putative power—*men at your feet, slave to your beauty and feminine wiles*—but ends up programming them as sexually disempowered women: the pleaser; in extreme form, the doormat.

All these dynamics mean that, when we think about consent, we're inevitably prone to think at the same time about these gender scripts. And when we read consent through such imbalanced and unfair scripts, the concept doesn't work as a pathway to good sex. Consent cannot successfully be framed as horny men making sure that women as asexual-but-slutty gatekeepers are saying yes. The classic gender norms for feminine and masculine sexuality limit and damage, for both men and women. Traditional masculinity and femininity make consent hard to ask for, hard to perceive, hard to give, and hard to withhold. The scripts muddy consent.

> "I recall researching 'How to give a blow job' for hours when I was a tween girl, because I had received the message loud and clear that the success of the sexual interaction depended on the male's sexual satisfaction. I also recall that it was a literal joke a few guys I knew in high school had: NEVER RECIPROCATE, they would yell at each other, laughing. I was in my fetal stages of feminism and asked why they harped on that so much. I think their answer basically had to do with the power dynamic—just phrased less intelligently."

> "The way we twist the narrative around rape for male and female victims are so vastly different, but so very similarly damaging. Girls who are sexually assaulted are not believed and are deemed sluts. Boys who are sexually assaulted are told it was not a big deal and their experiences are turned into a joke. Girls are demonized and boys are minimized, and both are hurt deeply in the process."

The good news is that, as the new gender and sexual revolution works its way through the culture, these scripts are changing. With the #MeToo phenomenon rewriting the rules about sex, the body positivity movement flourishing, and so many young people normalizing LGBTQIA+, we're in a process of moving beyond narrow and fixed norms of femininity and masculinity. We're breaking free and crafting new scripts. New guidelines for how to live a good life, how to experience and share pleasures of the body, and how to love. This cultural transformation offers room for people to live out a broader range of more authentic gender and sexual identity. It insists that sexuality be lived out consensually. More and more, people are challenging and changing the negative aspects of the gender scripts.

> "I do think that—in general—boys and men my age and younger are a lot smarter and more open about sex and gender than older ones, and this does give me hope."

As we undo and rebalance these harmful elements, the problem of consent begins to resolve. Consent gets closer to that original root meaning: *we feel together.* People become freer to be in touch with their desire, to articulate that desire in healthy ways with partners, and to feel their way together toward mutually desirable intimacy—instead of outcomes that are coerced or manipulative. We get closer to good sex.

The new lexicon terms undergirding this hopeful shift right now? *Toxic masculinity* and the *new inclusive masculinity.*

Chapter 17

BOYS DON'T
BELONG IN A BOX

It's important to spend some more time with the gender script of masculinity because—despite far-too-high rates of nonconsensual sexual encounters for *all* genders—sexual assault is still largely a crime of gender-based violence. Rape is committed most often by men and most often against women. The phrase "rape culture" refers to the normalization of sexual violence—to how prevalent and pervasive it is in society and to the low rate of its successful legal prosecution. This threat of sexual violence shapes women's lives, seething away in the background as a constant low-level hiss. Rape culture describes how dynamics of violence and domination are built into the very fabric of how we structure gender and sexuality and set up our society. It does not mean that society explicitly condones rape, which remains illegal, but that sexual misconduct is often trivialized, excused, even tolerated, and blamed on the victims themselves. It's about the sense of intimidation many women live with daily.

"Walking back to my dorm from dinner, I got catcalled three separate times by three different cars. I cannot help but feel extremely unsafe. It gives me hope to know that there are people out there working hard to challenge toxic masculinity."

"Much like other girls my age, I have had to deal with the aftermath of sexual assault, ranging from groping in bars to rape. Although I never pressed charges, rumors swirled around the school and I was confronted by multiple seniors claiming that I was lying to get attention."

A major source of rape culture is *toxic masculinity*. The term pops up a lot in recent media to describe the harmful parts of the traditional gender script for masculinity. If a guy's notion of masculinity—of how he acts out what he thinks it means to be a man—leads to harm to others or himself, then this notion constitutes toxic masculinity. Related phrases working their way into the popular consciousness are the "crisis of masculinity" and its positive flip term, the "new inclusive masculinity." The effort today is to rewrite the toxic aspects of the gender script of masculinity. Changing these notions can reduce sexual assault and result in other improvements to health and happiness for people of all genders.

This message is *not* male-bashing. To talk about toxic masculinity is not to say all guys are bad. It does not mean that masculinity as a gender role is bad. Nor is it saying that being a strong man is a bad thing. There are many good and noble values associated with traditional masculinity: protection of family, providing for others, courage, competence, self-reliance, ambition to succeed. The question at stake is how to encourage these values to manifest in positive ways and how to avoid the aspects that are detrimental to people's well-being.

Rape culture: According to the National Sexual Violence Resource Center, 81 percent of women and 43 percent of men in the US report having experienced some form of sexual harassment or assault. Only 25–40 percent of sexual assaults are reported to the police. And according to RAINN—the Rape, Abuse, and Incest National Network, which draws on the US Justice Department's annual *National Crime Victimization Survey* for its statistics—out of every one thousand sexual assaults, only twenty-five perpetrators will end up incarcerated.

"As a boy, from the minute I could walk, both of my parents would tell me that a man is supposed to be big, strong, tough, smart, and able to protect his family."

In 2018, the American Psychological Association (APA) took on this issue of toxic masculinity with a revised set of guidelines for health-care providers who work with boys and men. Their report created a splash. The APA presented evidence that if the goal is to improve the psychological and physical health of boys and men, then masculine gender norms must change. Health-care providers need to address and challenge these norms, because traditional masculinity is demonstrably harmful to male health.

This perhaps surprising message frames such masculinity as not only bad for women caught in rape culture and bad for society in general but bad also for the very men it is supposed to elevate. Rigid ideas of "manning up" hurt boys and men themselves. Truth is, guys suffer from the gender script—often more than they know and more than the culture has acknowledged. The big finding is that the more strictly you believe in the gender rules of the "Man Box"—another shorthand for restrictive gender ideals about male identity—the worse off you are as a guy.

A growing body of research and activism (see sidebar) links traditional masculinity to

> *Toxic masculinity,* as defined by *Oxford English Dictionary*: "A set of attitudes and ways of behaving stereotypically associated with or expected of men, regarded as having a negative impact on men and on society as a whole."

toxic side effects, not only to others around men, but to the men themselves. Men who align themselves with patriarchal norms commit violence against others at much higher rates. Examples of these norms include: "A man should not have to do household chores," "A real man should have as many sexual partners as he can," and "A man who talks a lot about his worries, fears, and problems shouldn't really get respect." The violence committed ranges from bullying and harassment to physical violence. Such men have higher rates of traffic accidents. They have lower rates of school com-

"*Promoting Healthy Manhood*": Promundo, a global consortium of nongovernmental organizations that focus on equitable gender relations and healthy masculinities, published *The Man Box* report in 2017. They partnered with academic researchers and with the Unilever men's grooming brand Axe to study how most young men worldwide "still feel pushed to live in the Man Box," in accordance with socially reinforced rules about how "real men" should behave. The *Man Box* term was first popularized by activist and educator Tony Porter, founder of the organization A Call to Men, who urged men in a 2010 TED talk (now with over three million views) to break free of the Man Box and shun toxic socialization to "act like a man."

pletion. They have poorer physical health outcomes, with more alcohol abuse and binge drinking—even lower rates of eating their vegetables. Their mental health suffers. Toxic masculinity puts guys at a higher risk of dying from suicide (at 3.5 times the rate of women), partly because dangerous gender myths such as "Depression is a sign of weakness" or "Feeling sad is not manly" make it harder for men to seek help. The core message to men here is clear: *Dude, toxic masculinity is bad for your health.*

Two injunctions are fundamental to this guy code of masculinity. The first is toughness, both physical and emotional. Guys are supposed to act tough and not look weak. It's a gender rule summed up in those phrases "He's the strong and silent type" and, especially, "Boys don't cry." This socialization toward stoicism inhibits and stunts the development of emotions associated with vulnerability and the feminine—such as sadness, fear, and worry—while overencouraging the expression of emotions deemed "manly"—primarily anger. Toxic masculinity imposes an emotional straitjacket on guys, a restriction of feeling that can lead to poor communication and relationship skills.

The second injunction of the tough-guy code is that the man is supposed to be sexual. Here's where toxic masculinity becomes particularly virulent for consent and good sex. A "real man" is a sexual player, a stud, and attracted to women—the traditional Man Box is pitifully homophobic. As part of their gender script, men are trained to be heterosexually assertive, even aggressive. Male desire is allowed free rein—a man is shamed, in fact, if he doesn't act sexual enough. A guy uninterested in sex risks having his masculinity called into question, evoking that laughable Hollywood figure of the forty-year-old male virgin. Toxic masculinity exaggerates and demonizes male sexuality, painting all guys as sex obsessed. It creates the notion of man as "sex fiend."

> "Even when I felt overwhelming sadness, I was so unable to process it that I couldn't cry. I *wanted* to cry in order to feel an emotional release, so I would watch sad movies or play sad songs to bring myself to tears and actually feel my pain. As a bisexual man with a fairly fluid gender expression, I usually feel confident I am not falling into the Man Box, yet I still find these small, nonsense rules conditioned within me that feed into the stupidness of toxic masculinity."

> "As a 22-year-old man, it is slightly embarrassing to say that I am still a virgin. It is not really a conscious decision that I have made, but I just have not met someone who I want to have sex with who also wants to have sex with me. I used to be very ashamed and self-conscious about the fact that I have never had sex."

These gender messages are doubled-edged for men: unfair and yet empowering. Yes, the Man Box traps boys in a tight fit that impedes full development and restricts range—*No tears, young lad, and better not wear pink or dream of becoming a ballet dancer or nurse, because we all know where that leads*—but the role accords power as well. The message of guys as hypersexual does harm by locking them into a narrow and dehumanizing script, but guys who buy into that script gain a certain cultural license for bad behavior. Others around the men then get hurt, while the men themselves have leeway to indulge their narcissism. The function of rape culture and male privilege—especially white and upper-class male privilege—means that men often get away with a lot. I'm not recommending we feel sorry for the rapist as a victim of his Man Box programming; obviously, lots of guys figure out consent and good sex.

> "Challenging the commonly held notion that men are horny monsters constantly seeking sex is very important. There have been moments where I assumed that maybe the man was not attracted to me, maybe they were a prude, maybe I was doing something wrong, but it was just my own bias that I assumed men wanted to have sex all the time. I mean, as a man, I know that *I* do not want sex all the time, but as a 'bottom' I guess I connected the extra masculinity I associate with 'tops' with the stereotypes that I have about hegemonic masculinity."

> "A Black man making a stupid drunk mistake at a bar could lead to something much worse happening to him than if a white guy did the same thing."

For some men, this guy code of hypersexuality makes trouble for consent: it can lead guys to believe their job is to convince women, to push past an initial no. After all, a strong man doesn't take no for an answer. Guys can get socialized into a sense of self where they pressure women because that's what they've been taught they have to do to be a man and to get respect in the culture. The Man Box valorizes power and dominance—even more so if the dominance is sexualized. This notion of men as supposed sex fiends contributes to sexual assault. When masculinity is coded as always up for sex, it justifies rape as almost an inevitability: *What do you expect? She was asking for it.*

> "The 'real man' façade makes boys more likely to endanger themselves, commit acts of sexual abuse, and be painfully lonely. But the status and privilege the 'real men' possess is noticed, and every boy grows up feeling they must achieve it to find themselves amongst the 'bros.'"

Male sexual violence—the violation of consent—exists in part because it's a way for men to demonstrate manhood within this twisted logic of toxic masculinity. A guy who thinks it's okay to have sexual contact with a woman passed out from intoxication is morally wrong, but the script that has convinced him it's okay is that of the Man Box. He sees an opportunity, the orgasm feels good, and the violation doesn't matter much because these things happen and she probably sort of deserved it anyway, by getting sloppy drunk and passing out in her short skirt and high heels at a late-night party. Such is the brutality of the Man Box. Even sexual assault of another man proves masculinity (and not impermissible same-sex desire) because of this pressure of the Man Box toward sexual mastery over another.

> "Basically, men were commonly acknowledged as hypersexual creatures powerless to control their urges. Girls got treated like they were responsible for provoking any unsought sexual behavior, because 'boys will be boys.' This perpetuates the idea that rape is a result of men's inherently overactive sex drive and cannot be helped."

This same pressure makes it hard for men to say no to sex. It also makes it hard for others—including women—to hear and take seriously men's refusal when they do say it. The point is important to the #MeToo movement and needs to be repeated: men are victims and survivors of sexual assault. In every class I teach, my male students report traumatized stories of unwanted touch, of coercion and badgering to have sex, of grooming and abuse by trusted adults when they were minors, of sexual assault when they were intoxicated at a party. Toxic masculinity contributes to these assaults, out of a sense that no "real man" would ever refuse sex and thereby fostering even more shame and silencing after the fact.

"I had an eighteen-year-old grope me when I was twelve. So, I can attest to the fact that extreme bullying occurs and that straight boys can and do sexually harass other straight boys out of a sense of power and domination."

"I do not think there is a reason other than societal programming making me believe men cannot be forced into sex. Despite my own non-consensual experiences, when two boys told me their first sexual experiences were non-consensual, I was confused. One was younger when it happened and his experience was with older girls, and the other was the same age as the girl but was drunk and did not want to have sex with her. I saw their pain, and they even explained how not even their closest friends knew these stories. I tried to comfort them, but I didn't actually understand how their story had caused them pain. I did not understand a world where a man could ever lack sexual agency. I think finally learning that a boner does not automatically equal interest or consent has helped me a lot. It also makes me rethink the ways I've gotten consent in the past, which I'm ashamed to say is something I never thought I needed to do. I think there is a bias in girls not only in thinking boys always want it, but also in being unable to imagine boys as vulnerable."

We need to dispel all these noxious messages, so many of them rooted in the relentless gender policing that young boys undergo. Boys are mocked, shamed, and bullied into meeting behavioral standards of masculinity. A high-stakes game to prove you're a man hurls hateful sneers and slurs against guys who can't or won't play by the rules. To embody ideal masculinity, guys have to avoid anything coded as traditionally feminine, which quickly earns censure as "gay." It's the male counterpart of the slut-shaming that girls endure: "Man up!" "Grow a pair!" "Don't be a pussy/wuss/sissy/fag!" Don't, in other words, be like a woman—the ultimate fail of manhood.

> "I always remember hearing 'Don't be a wuss' or 'Stop acting like a girl' whenever I would show emotion. It caused me to have a lot of built-up anger and it was not healthy. I used to always be teased by other kids about being 'gay' or a 'pussy' because my voice was higher than other boys, I didn't really act like them, and most of my friends were girls. My home life was not too bad, but my parents do have that traditional mindset that a man must provide and protect a woman and the woman must serve him. I am thankful that my girlfriend and I do not stand for those values and consider each other equal in our relationship."

> "Boys at my high school were so quick to call anyone, even their best friends, 'gay' for doing literally anything that wasn't manly. Anything from answering a question correctly in class, to being sad over a girl, to eating a salad for lunch. They also loved the phrase 'No homo.' Jocks at my school would literally say 'No homo' if they hugged their best guy friend."

Toxic masculinity is inculcated early on through these lessons received from family, school, peers, and media. That's one way violence gets normalized in society, through that old saying "boys will be boys." Boys, growing up, get caught in toxic gender scripts about masculinity, about what to do to be a man, to prove you're a real man. Good, kind, fun boys can get shamed and hardened by the culture into men who sometimes harrass, rape, and commit domestic violence, and who harm themselves as well. Guys learn to use power to dominate over others, including the domination of non-consensual sex. We don't want that to happen: for the sake of victims, but for the sake of those boys as well. No one is born a rapist.

> "When my boyfriend and I first started dating, he said his buddies would ask, 'Did you f*ck her?' every time after we hung out. Being a 'bro' meant you got laid each time you saw a girl. Thank goodness, that's not how my boyfriend was. His idea of being a man was being respectful and treating me as an equal."

How can boys and men take off the mask and drop the front of the tough guy to break free of norms of manhood that are not in their own best interests? In a way, the solution is simple: alter the script. Teach boys differently. Don't put boys in the Man Box. Let them grow up more freely—*Hey, buddy, wear pink socks if you want! Take up knitting instead of sports! Cry when you feel sad!* Let adults, especially adult men, act as role models by standing up against gender-based slurs and misogynist locker-room talk. Practice "bystander intervention," because silence is violence. Promote multiple modes of inclusive masculinities and stop insisting on one narrow and exclusive definition of manhood.

> "If, as a society, we did a better job of making a safe space for young boys to ask questions and feel comfortable being vulnerable, I think there would be a domino effect on everything else."

"To be a man, especially nowadays, it's more so intelligence and being a genuine person, instead of just being the big tough guy."

Such conversation is happening in the culture but in fits and starts. We live in a time when the script of masculinity is changing. Nowadays, there's more leeway to break down and open up gender roles. People have more options to keep the good parts, get rid of the bad parts, and make the script wider, more open to diversity. In America today, we are reimagining the meanings assigned to that damaging phrase "Be a man!"

"Penis size is not everything, and just because you're not part horse doesn't make you any less of a man."

In the end, the critique of toxic masculinity means there's more than one way to do your gender right. More than one way to define and embody masculinity. In fact, there are lots of ways to be a good man. Being gay is one of them. Being gender-nonconforming is one of them. If you can figure out heterosexual hypermasculinity without it violating gender equality or consent, then that way totally works too! (Rom-com heroes routinely pull off this act: alpha males who support their one-true-love in all things and never use violence except against the bad guys.)

"In my opinion, there is no one right way to be a man. There are many ways to be male. Men come in many different shapes and sizes. A man is not determined based on sexual organs or appearance or sexual orientation. It's about mutual understanding and respect for all people, who can embrace themselves for who they are."

This point is yet another example of how the denial of diversity creates problems—and of how a more inclusive approach resolves problems. When we center and affirm diversity from the get-go, we avoid harm in the first place. Toxic masculinity decreases as gender and sexual diversity are normalized.

Problem solved.

"Recently I've come out from the haze of Guyland, and it is so freeing."

Getting the gender scripts right helps people to consent—to agree through egalitarian communication—about the intimate relationships they desire. Such consent draws the line against bad sex. But we're aiming for a lot more than just avoiding bad sex.

Consent is our legal baseline and sets the groundwork conditions, but it's only the threshold. Absolutely necessary, but just the beginning.

"Yes, consent is a good thing, but a pat on the back for doing the bare minimum shows how far we have to go as a society to normalize and celebrate healthy and happy sexual lives for everybody."

No harm—a purely negative criterion—is not enough. We need positive criteria to get to good sex, let alone to great sex and the flourishing of human relationships.

We're ready now to celebrate desire and pleasure and love, in all their tingly glory.

Manisexto #5

SHARED PLEASURE

Good Sex Is Mutually Pleasurable and Respectful

Chapter 18

POWER WITH, NOT POWER OVER

We're almost there.

To review: in our moment of transformational cultural shift, the Manisexto gets us to (1) an ethical vision of positive sexuality, (2) an embrace of gender and sexual diversity, (3) inclusion of all bodies as good bodies, and (4) consent as sexy pillow talk, with the gender scripts to support it. With those elements affirmed, we approach the argument's climax. Only one piece is missing.

While the lessons of consent are crucial, they leave us wanting more than just negotiation to engage in a set of intimate activities. On the one hand, the more that's missing is *pleasure*: desire-soaked, bone-melting, volcano-erupting orgasmic pleasure, for all involved. On the other hand, the more is *love*: taking on forms ranging from respect and empathy, to affection and care, to the deepest of pair-bonded romantic commitment.

"Sex is supposed to be intimate and an important part of growth in a relationship but if it is just viewed as something you do to another person, that doesn't make it intimate at all and also you are just using one another."

We arrive, then, at the final element: (5) the centering of pleasure and love in power-with relationships. This vision leads away from the shame-and-blame gender tightrope and closes the orgasm gap through greater cliteracy and porn literacy. It even leads to a rhapsody on twenty-first-century love. Fundamental to this vision is thinking about sexuality, as well as relationship in general, in terms of *power with* instead of *power over*.

What is a power-with relationship, in the realm of sex and romance? It's one where an encounter with another nourishes and nurtures the participants. Where the flow of power is reciprocal and shared back and forth. Where the relationship is horizontal and egalitarian, so that partners meet each other's needs more or less equally. Power-over relationships, in contrast, are hierarchical in a problematic way that doesn't respect the needs and autonomous personhood of the partners. Instead of mutual respect, the flow of power is vertical and one-sided, exerted by one person over and against another.

> "I've thanked my mom because she always harped on the fact that she lost her virginity to someone she loved and with whom she was in a relationship. Without the words for it, my mom taught me about consent and mutual respect."

This problem of power-over relationships aligns with the problem of patriarchy and gender imbalance. As opposed to a cultural system that values the cooperative sharing of power with others, patriarchy values the competitive wielding of power over others: the tough guy stance, in other words. Patriarchy is a hierarchical system that encourages and rewards a power-over style of leadership. It is a system that valorizes control: control over one's body, over one's emotions, over people, over technology, over the environment. To gain such power over the other, intimidation and violence are often expected and tolerated—even glamorized (think of every Hollywood big-budget guns-and-explosion movie you've ever seen).

Power-over as an unhealthy form of relationship links up to patriarchy as an unjust cultural system, but the link is not absolute. While women have traditionally been less empowered and more vulnerable than men, women can exert unhealthy power-over in a heterosexual relationship with a man, just as they can adopt such a power-over style of action in the world. In fact, women who try to enact a more cooperative or collaborative style of leadership (in, for example, politics or the professional workplace) risk getting branded as "weak"—just as they risk labels of "pushy bitch" if they dare to step beyond the norms of femininity. In all cases, the name of the game remains patriarchy with the ultimate prize a form of control gendered as masculine. Although times have changed, America is still marked by such a system with its values of male-inflected, command-oriented power and with leadership positions still largely reserved for men.

Similarly, same-sex relationships, either lesbian or gay, and gender-nonbinary relationships can all be marked by unhealthy power-over dynamics. The common thread in all cases is the exercise of power to assert will and impose dominance over another person. The extent to which men themselves suffer from shaming, emotional straitjacketing, and brutality in this competition for power-over—as men with more power push those with less into lower-caste positions further down the hierarchy—demonstrates yet again how a patriarchal system imposes significant costs on men.

> "Guys are pressured by other guys to be the alpha and never to sink to beta. If this happens, respect is lost and you are considered a 'pussy' or a 'faggot.' It is 2021, and these norms are not gone."

> "I am currently talking to a boy and he is starting to get very vulnerable towards me; meanwhile, in group chats with our friends he acts all tough and everything is sexualized. He tells me he loves me and wants to be with me as his girlfriend, but he tells his friends that we're just friends with benefits. It is very frustrating, to say the least."

Part of why sex and relationships are complicated is precisely this system of patriarchy: a gendered structure of power-over that centers and privileges men and those qualities that the culture deems masculine, over and against women and those qualities deemed feminine. The inequities in personal relationships are mirrored at a larger scale by inequities at the sociocultural level. These structural inequities show up in the hierarchical patterns of racism, ableism, ageism, classism, heteronormativity, and other forms of discrimination. All these unjust systems function by privileging one group over and against another. The system of sexism grants men—particularly white, able-bodied, upper-class, heterosexual, cisgender men—more social power than women and feeds the imbalanced gender scripts.

> "We need to talk about the 'new masculinity': that the measurement of manhood isn't the number of sexual partners a man has had in the bedroom but the number of individuals he impacts in a positive way in the real world."

This point connects with the earlier discussion of rape culture: if masculinity wasn't so associated with power-over, if it wasn't so coded as being forceful and in charge over others, then rape and rape culture wouldn't be so pervasive. Sexual assault thrives in a sex-negative culture where sexuality gets tied up with gender scripts that value male dominance. Gender enacted for purposes of power-over is wrong, and sex used for purposes of power-over is wrong. Because of these twin convictions, inclusive masculinity champions the reciprocal style of the power-with relationship—empowering to all partners equally, no matter their gender identity.

> "The top video on the gay rendition of Pornhub today is titled: 'Tiny smooth twink fucked by older doctor during exam.' Most of the top video categories are depicting men of power overtaking someone younger and feebler than them. I used to not pay any attention to it, but the titles of these videos promote some of the most extreme ideologies."

Thinkers have long drawn versions of this contrast between power-with and power-over to make the point that the good life—"good" in our sense of both ethical and happy—involves egalitarian personal relationships. To mention three very different examples:

- Immanuel Kant, an influential eighteenth-century philosopher, talked about this ethics of relationship in terms of a "categorical imperative": the moral obligation to never treat or use other people solely as a means to an end, but always as an end in themselves. It functions in some ways as a universalizable version of the reciprocal golden rule found in many world religions to treat other people as you would wish to be treated yourself.

- Martin Buber, a Jewish scholar of the twentieth century, wrote a famous book contrasting the "I-Thou" and the "I-It" forms of relationship. His point is that we find meaning in life through genuine encounters in which we connect deeply with the other as a unique subject and not merely as an object to be used for some purpose.

- The late African American professor and cultural critic bell hooks developed a theory of love as a practice of action based in nurturing the growth of self and other. "The moment we choose to love," she writes, "we begin to move against domination, against oppression." In her feminist relational ethics, love is a caring practice of *freedom*, linked to the ability of communities to free themselves from oppression.

> "No one deserves to be treated like just some object or even to feel like that."

Each of these theories, despite their wide divergences, attests to the value of equity and mutuality in relationship. From them, implications emerge for healthy intimate connection: A good relationship is not asymmetrical. Sexual and romantic relationships are "good" when they embody norms of reciprocity. In such relationships, power is shared, decisions are made jointly, and there is negotiation and compromise. Students echo these ideas, saying consistently that what's most important is mutual trust, communication, and honesty. Behavioral guidelines for sex itself then follow, in terms of the standard of treatment we owe each other in an intimate power-with relationship.

> "We need to educate our society's parents and get them to start speaking with their children openly about sex. We need to talk about what it means to have a caring, respectful sexual and romantic partner."

First point up is mutual respect: treat your partner as more than simply a means to an end—whether that end be an orgasm, a sense of conquest, a higher social status, or a meal ticket. Treat them always as an end in themselves. Practice sharing power, with ongoing open communication. Eschew wielding power over other people. There are gradations of bad in how far sex might stray from this ideal of respect. Violent rape, for example, is worse than using someone for sex without concern for their feelings. But let's aim for the world we'd like to live in: a world where people are treated well, in and out of bed. Our own self-respect demands nothing less.

To put this point in the pithy terms of the vernacular: when you fuck someone, you shouldn't fuck with them. No lies, no mind games, no false promises, no leading them on. Good sex does not involve deception, exploitation, or manipulation. You don't take advantage of someone or prey on their vulnerabilities or insecurities just to get into their pants. Whether in the context of a casual hookup or a long-term married relationship, good sex is always fully consensual and respectful. Even an anonymous one-time encounter can model such respect. Similarly, sex can be kinky or rough, can play with fetishes or BDSM games of negotiated power exchange, yet still exemplify trust and mutuality. Despite practitioners' use of the terms *dominance* and *submission*, the enactment of BDSM top and bottom roles can be a form of healthy intimacy—and not of problematic power-over dynamics—when carried out with an empathetic commitment to the needs and flourishing of all partners.

Second up is mutual pleasure. If power is shared, gratification will be too. Equity in intimacy leads to the all-important *equity of pleasure*. Such equity means that good sex feels good for all involved. Mutual respect in a relationship ensures mutual pleasure in bed. The statement seems almost too obvious—that good sex will feel good—but this perspective on sex is quite radical in its departure from the reality that many people experience, especially women.

> "It's totally okay to be hooking up with people, but it needs to be a mutual experience where both people can openly communicate! Drinking alcohol to calm nerves and work up the courage to try something new might work in the moment, but it is not a long-term or healthy fix."

> "I think the best way for couples to both experience and reshape their ideas of 'pleasure' is to first develop mutual respect, both physically and emotionally."

I once invited a guest speaker to lecture in my Sexuality & Society class about cross-cultural perspectives on sex. He told the students, "A big reason people engage in sex is because it feels good, right?" A woman spoke up: "Sometimes," she said. To my ear, she sounded a little defiant, a little angry, but also wistful and sad. She was making an important, often ignored point: not everyone gets to enjoy sex. Women frequently miss out (more on that in chapter 20 on the orgasm gap).

> "I'm gay and not a part of heterosexual culture, but I know that on my side of things, mutual responsibility for pleasure is usually understood as shared. Here's hoping that culture continues to progress into a mutually beneficial world where people can learn and have fun while respecting each other's pleasure and boundaries."

Pleasure is important. It is not a frivolous or trivial thing. Sex-positivity argues that people have the right to their desire. The stance affirms sexual, bodily pleasure as a good thing—not a source of shame or guilt—for those who choose to engage in sex. Sensual delight comes in many forms—different, perhaps, for everyone. To know how your own body and its joys work—how to give and receive pleasure, in solo time by yourself and in a relationship—is fundamental. It functions as transformative self-knowledge. This aspect, too, of the American pursuit of happiness, the happiness of bodily sensation and carnal delight, is a basic human right.

> "Sex should be whatever you're comfortable with doing and something you enjoy. Not something that is acted out or done to please another person."

This equity of pleasure springs from the equity of desire. Not the *equality* of desire—a false universal claim that all people experience the same amount of the same sort of desire—but the notion that everyone has an equal right to enjoy the experience of their own consensual desire. In the past, this right has been denied, for example, to queer, lesbian, and gay people, as well as to many people with disabilities. To repeat: everyone has the right to access their sexual pleasure. But we also need to insist: no one has the right to a sexual partner against another person's will. The dark-alley rapist, the child molester, the smooth-talking groomer of the teenage runaway, the workplace harasser demanding sex favors or else, the angry online incel—such people are enacting violent power-over relationships, and *none* of them have the right to impose their desire on anyone else.

A word also about orgasm. In celebrating pleasure, we don't want to become overly *climax centered*. The Manisexto issues no mandate for number of required orgasms per sexual encounter. Positive sexuality endorses a wider definition of what constitutes good sex than the "happy ending" of an orgasm. The expectation that intimacy must always be orgasmic is a stressful pressure. Not reaching climax can become a reason to feel like a failure, particularly for younger people still figuring out how their sexuality works and what brings them or a partner to orgasm, and especially for women already shamed by the culture for feeling any desire at all (*You dirty slut*, sneers a voice in the back of many a gal's mind).

By itself, orgasm is not the only or even best definition of good sex. Its sensation of climax and release generally feels great, but good sex does not equal an orgasm. A person can have what they consider to be good sex without climaxing. They may be having sex for other reasons that make sense for them, such as experimentation, gaining experience, curiosity, practice, feeling close to a partner, pleasing a partner, or keeping a relationship strong. Alternately, a person can experience an orgasm against their will during a sexual assault, as the body responds despite itself (a source of cruel and unnecessary shame for rape survivors).

"Intimacy is far more than an orgasm."

Sex doesn't always have to be orgasmic, but it should certainly bring pleasure. Everyone should be having fun, with enjoyment all around—and not the forced pleasure of unwanted arousal. Intimacy should feel good. "Good" here includes the widest range of bodily pleasures, as well as positive emotions such as feeling happy, confident, cared for, valued, and safe. All that counts. Intimacy should be free of negative emotions such as guilt, shame, fear, and disgust. If the encounter feels satisfying for all partners, however they define satisfaction of their desire and whether or or not it includes orgasm, then what the partners are doing is right for them.

Good sex is intimacy in the context of power-with relationships that is mutually respectful and mutually pleasurable. The goal, as sociologist of hookup culture Dr. Lisa Wade puts it, is to envision "sexualities that are more authentic, kinder, safer, more pleasurable, and less warped by prejudice, consumerism, status, and superficiality."

With these norms in place, we can take one last pass through the gender scripts to ask a crucial question for the goal of shared pleasure in healthy intimacy: what would it take for everyone to feel good?

Chapter 19

WHO GETS TO FEEL GOOD?

Gender and Pleasure beyond the Shame-and-Blame Tightrope

With all the toxicity wrapped up in the traditional gender scripts—their chokingly tight fit for so many—why do the old norms endure and hold such sway? Why do my students, for example, still report witnessing so much adherence to the gender scripts even as they readily—even bitterly—criticize them?

Partly, it's because of the human need for a sense of identity, both as an individual and as part of the larger society. On one's own, it's hard work to craft a healthy sense of self. It can seem easier to latch onto ready-made cultural tropes: the manly man or the girly girl, for example. As a young person growing up amid the confusions of adolescence and the hormonal surges of puberty, the appeal can be strong for someone to just hand us a script that tells us how to act out our gender and sexual identities. Play this part, become this person, and you are guaranteed a place in society.

Such set roles will never work for certain people (especially those in marginalized gender and sexual minority groups) and will always come at some cost for everyone, but if you can play along, at least such a system tells you who you are and what is expected of you. It addresses people's need for identity and belonging. It provides an answer, acceptable to that majority culture, about the conundrums of being human.

There's a more painful reason why people continue to accept inculturation into the gender scripts: the cost of refusal is high. People who don't do their gender or sexuality "right" according to the accepted norms are shamed, often brutally, through the function of powerful regulatory mechanisms in the culture. In essence, the scripts force people to walk a tightrope, hewing to the narrowest possible range of gender roles, and punish both men and women with shame-and-blame dynamics when they inevitably tumble off.

The questions become: How do we ensure that gender functions to create meaningful and positive options for identity and belonging that do not become oppressive or toxic? How do we play with gender (because man caves, goddess cocktail hour, bro rituals, and bachelorette hen parties can be a whole lot of fun) in ways that are creative and supportive of individual difference and that do not turn into punitive one-size-must-fit-all boxes mandated for everyone?

For the goal of equitable erotic pleasure, these questions are central. That's because the old gender scripts—men as horny sex monsters, women as Madonna/whore gatekeepers—not only muddy consent. They also block equal access to pleasure.

> "Men feel that women are emotional beings who love being enchanted by a tough, athletic, lady killer, while many women find that guys are sex-crazed, unemotional creatures from the barbaric times."

So, how do we ensure that gender norms support equity in bed—of everybody getting to feel good when it comes to sex? In short, how can we live gender off the shame-and-blame tightrope?

The current moment actively explores this question with new visions of gender, bold forays into gender fluidity and nonbinary gender subjectivities, and inclusion for sexual diversity. Today, we have a better sense than ever before of the injustices of the gender scripts. People are actively writing themselves new scripts that feature greater flexibility and liberty to live an authentic life.

New male subjectivities, often modeled first by celebrities and within youth culture, experiment with different styles of masculinity: androgynous, metrosexual, urban hipster, lumbersexual, spornosexual.

Let's think first about guys.

The new masculinity, while offering freedom from the confines of the Man Box, can ironically make guys feel like they're caught anew. The fresh trap is a tricky highwire balancing act. Men need to pull off a workable style of masculinity somewhere between the older and the more capacious contemporary gender scripts. You can't be too old-school tough guy, but you can't be too touchy-feely sensitive either.

> "There's a paradox I've witnessed in my friend groups and personal relationships. Girls want their partners to open up to them and not be such a tough guy. Some think that it is 'cute' when guys cry. However, there is a very delicate balance between opening up and being too emotional, in their eyes. I believe that this situation only further complicates things, because now, their significant others have to walk a tightrope of how much to share in their relationship, putting those guys in a very similar situation as with their male friend groups."

There may be more than one way to be a good man these days, but the irony of the shame game persists as society adapts to these new norms. Men are encouraged by our moment of cultural transition to be more emotionally open but can be mocked and shunned by both men and women around them when they do open up.

Try looking at it from the perspective of your average heterosexual guy. All too often, he receives little to no real sex education at school, his parents never talk to him much about sex, pornography is his main source for learning what sex looks like, and the Man Box tells him he needs to be dominant and a sexual player. When he tries to open up to girlfriends and admit he's scared or clueless about sex—scared or clueless about anything, really—there's a good chance one of them tells him to "grow a pair." Or they're simply confused by that un-boxed male and not sure how to respond to him. All that because women have been exposed to the very same toxic programming that defines a good man as stoic and masterful.

"When I was young, it was always macho stuff between me and my other guy friends. Showing any emotion other than happiness or anger really was showing weakness, and we pounced on one another to condemn such things. Then I met a girl and the second I showed other emotions she was glad and accepting of me for it . . . but the more I did that, it's like red flags went off for her. If I was too emotional, it scared her, or she didn't like it. She called me a pussy and told me to man up. I was better off with the boys. At least they would have shut me down quick, not let me open up and become vulnerable and then stab me in the heart."

"As a woman, after thinking about my own perception of masculinity I realized I still hold some old-fashioned views. I don't know how to react when a boy cries in front of me. I want to support them, but it is so foreign to me that I don't know what to do."

In our moment of cultural transition, a guy trying to emerge from the Man Box is easily shamed right back into it.

"When I hear my gal friends define the guy they want to marry, they want him to be athletic, powerful, rich, and good-looking. We want to change the limited ideas about being a woman, but we won't let go of these outdated ideas of what it should mean to be a man."

Guys can end up feeling like they're walking a gender tightrope, a razor-thin line where it's far too easy to stumble and fall to either side. In the quest for good relationships and a healthy sexual sense of self, they can end up feeling damned if they do, damned if they don't.

Guess what? It's how women have always felt.

> "Young men are faced with a choice: they can either continue their practices in order to fit in with the other guys or they must outcast themselves from the population of 'real men.' Anything a man says that emits feelings, changes the status quo, or even makes the rest of the bros question their differences can cause him to be seen as a 'little bitch.'"

Guys caught in the new double bind—be sensitive but somehow still sexy bad-boy tough and not *too* much of an emotive nice guy—are experiencing a version of the old double bind that has long trapped women within the equally contradictory messages that they have to be sexy but somehow still pure. Both genders now face the problem of navigating these traps in their respective scripts.

> "In today's society, if you don't give in to men, you're considered a prude, and if you hook up with them then you're a whore. There's no in between. I think as women we need to stop living up to the unrealistic sexual standards set by men in a 'man's world.'"

Girls and women get twisted up in this bind and subjected to painful double standards. My female students talk about it *all the time* as a central and maddening feature of the gender scripts (actually, lots of the guys notice it also and sympathize). What the girls discover, early on, is that they're caught in a no-win situation. They're taught, trained by the scripts, to look and act sexy for boys. Simultaneously, they're taught that their own desire is shameful and that wanting sex—prioritizing their own sexual pleasure—is wrong. You have to be sexy, or you're dismissed and shamed as a prude, as an "uggo," as no fun. But when you *are* sexy—especially if you dare to be sexual for yourself, to claim the right to your sexual agency and satisfaction—you're dismissed as a whore. A woman's body is coded as sexy but not sexual: she's not allowed to enjoy the sexuality she is required to project. She exists more as a sexual object than a sexual subject. In extreme cases of human trafficking, more as a sexual slave than an autonomous sexual citizen.

"The more I said no, the more he asked, and the more I was called a prude by those around me."

The infamous and cruel double standard kicks in, the one that allows men to get away with the sort of sexual player behavior that gets women condemned. Girls are held to behavioral guidelines that guys aren't and are shamed for activity that guys can carry off with impunity or even praise. We disdain women for becoming what the gender script makes them.

Where is the possibility for the equity of shared pleasure amid such impossible mixed messages? How's a gal to avoid getting branded a slut for doing what earns him a high five as a player? Be Madonna and whore at the same time. Again: damned if you do, damned if you don't. The bind suffocates. It stunts the healthy development of a girl's sexual sense of self.

Unless we change some of these scripts.

"It is very much ingrained into our culture that women and girls are sexual objects, existing to please men, but if they have sex or perform sexual acts they are shamed. It is very interesting, because girls having sex is simply a well-attuned response to all the socialization they experience telling them to do so."

No wonder that women, more so than men, have difficulty accessing pleasure in heterosexual relationships. Guys receive greater cultural encouragement to exist as sexual beings. They have higher rates of masturbation. They enjoy greater permission to explore the world; they're expected to be assertive, even aggressive. Girls, on the other hand, already sense that sex is scarier and higher stakes for them, disadvantaged as they are by rape culture, the imbalanced gender scripts, and their assigned gatekeeper role. Women are more vulnerable to sexual assault, subject to unwanted pregnancy, and all too aware of the slut-shaming they risk if they dare articulate their own desire.

> "Women are constantly slut-shamed for literally anything and everything they do, and it's not only men shaming us. My grandma, for example, shames my clothes if they're too revealing, shames me if I don't sit with my legs crossed for not being 'lady like,' shames me for wearing too much makeup or dyeing my hair—the list goes on. Women are shamed if they have a high body count or date a lot of men, while men are praised for it. Yet, if women don't put out, they're boring. We just cannot win."

In sexual situations, before you can consent to anything, you ideally need to know whether you want what's on offer. While this may sound simple, it is not an easy task. It's especially challenging for women, who are often socialized to attend to the needs of others before their own. Women can have great difficulty identifying and expressing what they want sexually when they've been raised to prioritize the pleasure of others. Women, still today, are often trained into the greater compliance and docility of the "nice girl" stance, the pleaser who is taught to make others happy. Women are trained by the culture to seek and expect romantic love but not to seek or expect their own sexual pleasure.

> "Female sexual pleasure is elusive because we condition it to be so. Many girls are not even aware that sex *can* result in pleasure for them, because masturbation for girls is considered gross and taboo."

I once had a friend whose mother told her, as part of a set of instructions for how to behave at a school social event, that if a boy asks you to dance, you have to say yes. "If he got up the courage to ask, don't you dare tell him no," were her mother's words. It didn't matter if you wanted to dance with the boy or not. It didn't matter if you liked or disliked the particular boy who asked. The girl's desire, in other words, should play no role in her decision: if he wanted it, she had to say yes.

"Women are made to feel like their purpose during sex is to look good and make a guy feel good. Women have that narrative ingrained in their brains."

In all these ways, traditional notions of femininity become toxic to women's knowledge about their own erotic pleasure. The notions work against women's sexual gratification. They undercut women's sense of sexual agency. Sexual passivity can then follow. She says yes when she'd really rather not. She gives him the blowjob and doesn't expect oral sex in return. She accepts that sex is over once he reaches climax, even if she hasn't.

"There is a general shame that many women feel when asking for pleasure. They feel bad and inconsiderate for also wanting to orgasm, so they don't talk to their partners about their needs. Women would prefer to give rather than receive. I feel that a lot of this has to do with wanting to avoid the judgement of something they desire."

"To grow up queer and alone is to believe that your pleasure and the way you have sex is invalid, to believe that your desires are wrong. I remember the first time my mom told me what sex was she said, 'It is when a man enters himself into a woman.' During a discussion with a group of girls who had only experienced straight sex, they revealed to me sex wasn't real until there was penetration. I wondered what they thought lesbians like me did. I felt ashamed. But I also found myself more and more confused as to why women would want to hook up with anyone whose goal wasn't to make them orgasm."

Given these toxic scripts of feminine sexuality, given their deadening effect on women's sexual pleasures, it is neither realistic nor fair to expect women to advocate easily for their own needs in bed. How is a woman to even recognize her desire? From the point in time when she makes her sexual debut—an expression more consistent with positive sexuality than the fraught and fearsome phrase "lose your virginity"—she's deprived of the vocabulary and cultural support to articulate and enact that desire.

Step one, then, toward the goal of the equity of pleasure is for women to get in touch with their desire. Often literally—masturbation is a great place to start to figure out how your body works and what sort of stimulation you enjoy. What feels good to you? What are your limits and boundaries about what you *don't* want?

> "I think by not emphasizing that women should prioritize their needs in bed just as much as their partners, we are contributing to this idea that women should be ashamed of their sex drives or their desire for pleasure."

The new sex-positive messaging—counter to the old shame-and-blame double-bind messaging—is to *own your desire*. Connect with it, deeply. Explore its contours. Learn to recognize the feel, the shape, the pulse of your desire moving through your body. Know that the desire is *yours*, a precious gift of embodiment, that its purpose is to make you feel good, and that these feelings are a good thing. Your sexual pleasure is *not* shameful but is part of the sweetness and joy of life.

> "Even powerful women are made to feel like they should be docile in the bedroom. Until recently, I was like this. I am very outspoken in all aspects of my life. I'm known for being honest at all costs. And even me, in the bedroom, found myself lying about experiencing pleasure and putting my needs second so as to not embarrass myself and not embarrass my partner. Being 'bad at orgasming' is embarrassing!"

Step two is to feel comfortable expressing this sense of positive sexuality, if you're in a situation where you've chosen to be with a partner. And that might be even harder. To feel entitled to your desire and then to be able to articulate that desire to someone else—*I like to be touched there, slower, faster, now, how about we try this?*—is a difficult challenge, indeed. The message here is to moan out loud a lusty and affirmative *Yes!* to the sex you do want, that you crave. (Remember that line about how a lady isn't supposed to raise her voice? Fuck that, literally.)

> "It is dangerous to suppress the sexual desires and needs of women. It is taking away our voice and our power. It is continuing to let men silence us."

Woman, man, or gender-nonbinary: know you are entitled to sexual pleasure—either by yourself or with consensual partners. Learn how to claim for yourself a healthy intimate relationship. Believe, shame-free and down to your bones, that you have the right to live out your *Yes*.

> "It makes me feel so much better now that I know my own worth. I don't allow anyone to treat me like I'm just some object. There were many instances before where I found myself not saying no because I was afraid. I did not want to upset the guy I was with, which is absurd. I risked my own comfort to not make the guy upset and to save his feelings. I refuse to ever do that again. Over the last three years, I have learned so much about myself and grown into an adult. The one that knows she is an amazing person, demands the respect that she deserves, and does not take any mess from anyone."

You don't have to let society's expectations, the pressures of an unloving partner, or disempowering internalized notions program your sexuality for you. It's okay to say no to the sex you don't want, the sex that doesn't feel good and that isn't mutually respectful and loving. It's also okay—really okay—when you're having sex you do want, to advocate for your fullest pleasure. This is the challenge of sexual agency: to develop your voice and to acknowledge and embrace your desire.

"Rather than being slut-shamed as a woman, or love-shamed as a male, we should focus on normalizing young adults' sexual experiences and desires. We should change the way we have 'the talk' to be an ongoing conversation about sexual pleasure, respect for partners, and what exactly consent looks/sounds like."

None of this is easy. It requires self-knowledge, self-esteem, strong communication skills, and emotional maturity. It requires courage. Desire is a slippery beast to grasp.

But it feels damn good when you do.

Chapter 20

CLOSING THE ORGASM GAP

Porn and Hookups

Did you know there's an "orgasm gap"?

Men have more orgasms than women. The shame-and-blame gender tightrope leads us straight into this gap, this trap, through its dampening of women's sense of sexual agency. In heterosexual sex—particularly one-night-stand hookup sex and encounters early on in a relationship—the guys are more likely to climax by up to a 3:1 ratio. That means those male partners have three orgasms for every one that the women experience.

> "By being a man, I have so many privileges that I don't realize—one of them being I have never not had an orgasm from a sexual encounter."

This orgasm gap does not exist in gay or lesbian sex, and the gap can shrink to almost nothing for long-term heterosexual couples who engage in a wide range of stimulation practices (for example, oral sex and fingering, as well as penetration). As sociologist Lisa Wade reports, the problem is not that the female orgasm is elusive or "finicky." The lesbian couples man-

Learn more about the orgasm gap and female sexual response in the work of sociologist Lisa Wade, *American Hookup: The New Culture of Sex on Campus* (2017) and science philosopher Elisabeth Lloyd's *The Case of the Female Orgasm: Bias in the Science of Evolution* (2006).

age just fine, as do women masturbating on their own—an average of "just four efficient minutes" to climax in solo sex.

So why, in heterosexual casual sex, do women tend to have fewer orgasms than men? A big part of the problem is the lack of "cliteracy"—literacy about the clitoris—or a general lack of knowledge about women's sexuality, on top of the failure we've seen by the culture to value and authorize female sexual pleasure to the same degree that it does male pleasure. This problem relates to an overemphasis on penis-in-vagina penetration as the definition of what constitutes sex. (More on all that in the next chapter.)

"What does it mean to have pleasurable intercourse? Why isn't sex as great as everyone hypes it up to be?"

As for solutions, we've already noted the importance of widening the gender and sexual scripts for people of all genders, to make these notions more inclusive and equitable and to decrease negative shaming dynamics. But work on another front is needed to help achieve the goal of mutual shared pleasure. To crack the gendered politics of climax and achieve orgasm equality, we've got to take on pornography and hookup culture.

"Changing the culture changes the porn."

One reason for the orgasm gap—as well as for other current aspects of bad sex—is porn. Pornography is incredibly accessible nowadays, much more so than in generations past. Thanks to the ready availability of digital devices and high-speed internet, it's easy to go online and surf a huge array of free porn sites.

Such pornography is not all bad, nor is this ubiquity necessarily a bad thing. The mainstreaming of porn, including amateur porn, is part of the new gender and sexual revolution. Such "pornification" of the culture has its advantages: more openness about sex, less stigma around it, and less shaming about consensual sexual desires outside the "vanilla" standard (heterosexual, married, male-led, missionary position, reproductive, etc.). Porn helps bring conversations about consensual kinks and fetishes into the mainstream.

> "I am thankful to porn for kind of mainstreaming kink culture, but the problem is that people have romanticized it and think that kink or rougher sex is the only option. It's OKAY to be 'vanilla' or like missionary only or not want to have sex that often. I think people just need to be more comfortable vocalizing their preferences and have confidence they will find a partner whose sexuality matches up with theirs."

New sex-positive queer and feminist porn, sometimes called "ethical porn" (yes, that's a thing! And we need more of it!), radically widens on-screen representation of people enjoying sex. In such alternative porn, people of color, people with disabilities, people of size, people who don't conform to gender norms or typical styl-ing norms (which may simply be a gal who doesn't shave her pubic hair) can all be represented on-screen and work in adult entertainment production, not fetishized into the exotic other or a freak show, but honestly presenting a wider narrative about sexual pleasure and possibility.

Annie Sprinkle in "God Breast America" by Julian Cash. Photo credit: Julian Cash.

> **Porn literacy** is a form of media literacy focused on pornography. Porn literacy curricula—often aimed at young people—teach critical thinking skills and ethical analysis about the role of porn, its impact on people's understanding of sexuality, and the potential limitations inherent in porn's representation of healthy and reciprocal intimacy. See, for example, porn literacy programs by the Boston Public Health Commission (featured in the **New York Times**) and the Toronto Teen Health Source.

There's a convincing movement of feminist, queer, and ethical porn that argues, in the words of Annie Sprinkle (sex work pioneer and one of the original sex-positive feminists) in *Hardcore from the Heart*, that "the answer to bad porn is not no porn, but to make better porn!" Check out also, for example, Tristan Taormino et al., editors, *The Feminist Porn Book: The Politics of Producing Pleasure* (2013).

Here's what *is* bad. Due to the lack of high-quality and comprehensive sex education in schools across America, many young people end up getting much of their sex education through pornography. Not the alternative ethical porn but the more commonly available mainstream—or malestream—porn. Such porn becomes the default sex ed, a function for which porn is not intended, camera-ready forbidden fantasy factory that it is. Porn is not meant to be realistic. And most porn—this statement may not surprise you either—is not very cliterate. It's often, in fact, demeaning toward women (as well as toward people of color), and its focus is mainly on men's pleasure.

The very language of porn reveals this bias: the iconic porn term *the money shot* refers to the essential scene of male ejaculation. The visual proof of a man's orgasm serves as the cinematographic climax of a porn clip, as well as the sexual climax of the action. Once you've got that crucial shot, the porn video is over, and the sex is over. "Money shot" enters the vernacular as that element of a situation or narrative that is most impressive, most visually impactful, most powerful—the *Wow!* moment. It's what you've been waiting for, building to, the whole point of why you're there—and all based on the theatrics of male orgasm.

Given the influence of pornography, we need better porn literacy. Teens in particular need more critical awareness about the role of porn, its impact on people's understanding of sexuality, and the limitations inherent in porn's representation of healthy and reciprocal intimacy. And in order to address the orgasm gap and embody the goal of shared pleasure through orgasm equality, we need to think about hookup sex.

These casual, one-off encounters are the realm of sex most like porn: relatively anonymous, about the moment, about physical pleasure more than emotional investment (what the students call "catching feelings"), with partners largely viewed as interchangeable. Hookup sex among young people often follows porn tropes, including the centering of male sexual desire and the prioritizing of male orgasm. That's why hookup culture and porn culture are intertwined in this problem of the orgasm gap. Sex in both realms can end up as asymmetrical and lacking in cliteracy. The way my students (who want to talk about the problems of porn and hookup culture *a lot*) put it? It shouldn't all be about going to "Pound Town."

"It's a FACT that younger people today see porn and think that's how they are supposed to have sex. I see this to be true and hear about it from my peers. From the aggressive manner, to the female vocalizing, to the male ejaculation being the 'end' of the sexual encounter. And the point about men cumming on women's faces: porn teaches that all men love it, all women love it, so we must pretend to love it, too. I have even thought about this with respect to myself—how much of my sexual interactions are performative because of what I have seen in porn? Hopefully not a lot anymore—LOL!"

"As a female college student, it is obvious to me that the desire of the average Joe to have anal or rough sex is exacerbated by the porn industry making it seem commonplace."

Hookup culture, like porn itself, is not all bad and has its positive aspects. No-strings-attached sex can be a way to explore and experiment, to break free of the moralizing one-size-fits-all sexual scripts.

> "I've always been very supportive of casual sex. I see it as an act of rebellion against traditional, rigid, and 'acceptable' sexual norms imposed on my generation. It's one's own right as an act of total body autonomy."

For women and people who identify as queer, hookups can be a form of protest against discriminatory taboos. Women, for example, may engage in casual sex to reclaim their right to define sexuality on their own terms. As Wade writes in her sociological study *American Hookup*, "Young women have embraced this new reality; they are no longer willing to play the angel to men's frisky devil. They flatly reject the idea that they should be our society's moral compass, especially in college." Some women use hookups as a way to fight back against the narrowness and double standards of the sexual scripts.

> "When I got to college, I decided to hook up with strangers (I didn't want to hook up with people I knew because I didn't want to have to worry about their feelings). Part of that was because I grew up as a girl with three brothers in a very small, very Midwestern, very red town, and I was painfully aware of how the patriarchy worked. I decided that my way of fighting the patriarchy was to treat men the way they treated women. And that worked for me."

For a lot of people, of all genders, the hookup experience is mixed. They derive some sense of enjoyment from it—physical, social, or emotional—but they feel ambivalence as well. They sense they're motivated less by their own desire and more by a set of peer pressures and cultural pressures to conform to an expected sexual script: the woman as the pleaser who gives sex, the man as the player who takes sex. While these pressures differ, they exert great weight in both cases and lead to iffy consent scenarios.

"Women often see intercourse or even oral sex as a way to feel desired or a way to boost social status. I felt the need to prove myself through intimacy with men. I do not know that I ever actually had the desire to be intimate with a man, but my friends were all doing it and it made me feel insecure that I was the only one who had not participated. Looking back, it wasn't too enjoyable at all; however, in the moment, it made me feel less insecure and more equal with my friends."

"As a guy, I know many of my male friends have felt forced into doing intimate things that they weren't comfortable with at the time because the girl acted like 'Oh, of course a guy would want to do it' or because they felt they were just supposed to be okay with it because they were a guy."

The realm of the heterosexual one-night stand is also where my women students become very familiar with the orgasm gap. It's something they experience routinely. Hookup culture permits—makes almost inevitable by its very setup—all sorts of one-sided sex. Despite the gains of gender equity in the present day, the hookup scene remains a site of power-over relationship and male pleasure. It's where the guys come and the women don't.

"A hookup is inherently the opposite of intimacy. You aren't allowed to act too interested. You aren't allowed to kiss too much or cuddle after. It's from Point A to Point B (which usually means the guy using the girl to masturbate)."

Sometimes, women resent the imbalance of the encounter and demand more pleasure for themselves. As one student bluntly said, "I'm not your cum dumpster." Women can feel like the guy is using them to act out a porn script.

> "In my early college years, I would just hook up with guys and felt like I had to make sure they were pleasured and they were able to finish. I had no problem giving oral sex, I honestly genuinely enjoy it, but I almost feel like guys view that as an automatic given that you have to do. On the flip side there is no automatic given that a guy would give oral to a girl. I've had guys say they don't like to give oral to girls, or it goes straight from the girl giving oral to the guy and then onto penetration, which is totally unfair to the woman. I feel like women's sexual needs are not a priority for most men during sex."

These dynamics are not only heterosexual and not only disempowering to women. Sex can be bad for the guys too—even with an orgasm. Hookup culture can end up feeling joyless and hollow across the gender and sexuality spectrum—ironically sex-negative instead of sex-positive.

> "As a gay man, I recently had to get out of hookup culture. The damage it did to my own psyche really outweighed the sexual pleasure. There is little to no conversation; I have a habit of looking at the wall and not making a personal connection. I kept on hooking up with others to feel that kind of 'thrill,' but it wasn't until recently that I realized I need to have a personal connection with my partner to fully enjoy the sex."

I don't mean to imply that casual sex is immature, a phase that some young people pass through on their way to longer-term relationships. Hookups *can* be mutually pleasurable and respectful, as an ongoing style of serial intimacy shared with a range of partners. The tricky part is to realize that possibility and not to evade it. As journalist Peggy Orenstein puts it in *Girls & Sex: Navigating the Complicated New Landscape*, "The question to me, then, became less about whether hookups were 'good' or 'bad' for girls than about how to ensure reciprocity, respect, and agency regardless of the context of a sexual encounter."

> "As a guy, I see how I have used casual sex as a way to not hold myself accountable to being a fair, respectful, and equitable sexual partner. Examples of this include not caring if the other person had an orgasm, ghosting them after a sexual encounter, or being rude because I cared more about getting my nut in than I did being a genuine and nice human being. That's the mentality I had from hookup culture: license to be unkind. It gave me access to virtually unlimited partners, through apps like Tinder and Grindr, until I no longer saw them as people but more so as disposable sex toys I had the ability to call upon and dismiss at will. I'm now able to realize how harmful my actions were to other people, as well as to my own emotional intelligence and ability to form meaningful connections."

So: holding oneself accountable to being an "equitable sexual partner," whether it's for a night or for a lifetime.

We're ready now to improve our cliteracy.

Chapter 21

CLITERACY AND THE POLITICS OF PLEASURE

To talk about the clitoris is to say that women's sexual satisfaction matters.

To even use that word—*clitoris*, the *clit*, the only human organ devoted solely to pleasure—is to change the conversation around sexuality to make equal room for discussion of female erotic gratification. When I get the students talking about it, they gleefully suggest the phrase *Going to Clit City* instead of Pound Town.

To then introduce the term *cliteracy*—literacy about the clitoris, a savviness about women's sexuality—is to speak a truth that is silenced and suppressed by the traditional cultural scripts about gender and sexuality. The truth: female sexual pleasure centers on the clitoris. It is to shift discourse away from a vagina to be penetrated to a clitoris to be stimulated. Ultimately, it is to affirm women as full and equal sexual citizens.

Here's the thing: penetration doesn't work for most women. It is not a reliable pathway to climax. The problem, at its core, is that vaginal intercourse favors male orgasm. Penis-in-vagina sex quite reliably brings heterosexual men to orgasm. Less so heterosexual women.

According to numerous science-based studies, only about 25 percent of women consistently reach orgasm from vaginal penetration alone. Much more consistently, what brings more women the most pleasure—and what leads most easily to female orgasm—is stimulation of the clitoris. Over 90 percent of women who masturbate do so with little or no vaginal penetration, concentrating on clitoral stimulation instead. As sex educator Dr. Emily Nagoski puts it, "The clitoris really is the hokey pokey." That's what it's all about.

> "In sex ed, there was very little discussion about pleasure but even less so about female pleasure. When filling out the vaginal diagram, I am quite sure the clitoris was left out. The clit has nothing to do with reproduction and therefore it's removed as insignificant. I am appalled that we live in a society where male pleasure is the determinant of sex and I have many questions for my straight friends."

Improve your cliteracy with recent books such as psychologist Laurie Mintz's *Becoming Cliterate: Why Orgasm Equality Matters—And How to Get It* (2017) and sexual-health expert Emily Nagoski's *Come As You Are: The Surprising New Science That Will Transform Your Sex Life* (2021). Learn about the "politics of feeling good" with *New York Times* best seller adrienne maree brown's *Pleasure Activism* (2019).

Time to start reclaiming the politics of pleasure. Doing so means that those people who've been shut out of experiencing sensual delight regain access to the pleasures of which their bodies are capable. The gender and sexual scripts have encouraged a disconnect in women from the full pleasures of their bodies, as much as in men from the full range of their emotions. Neither result is good. In an ideal world, children of all genders are allowed to develop into whole human beings, encouraged to connect fully with the goodness of their bodies and the depth of their emotions. In an ideal world, society respects the rights of all bodies to feel good. That's the world of the Manisexto.

Greater cliteracy addresses the heterosexual orgasm gap caused by the problems of power-over relationships, by shaming and double standards in the gender and sexual scripts, and by one-sided porn and hookups. The lesson of cliteracy is to close that orgasm gap through less emphasis on the penis as the magic wand of pleasure and on penetration as the means of pleasure delivery.

> "Even in media representations of heterosexual sex, the female actors will usually overemphasize the pleasure they are receiving from seemingly just the penetration from the male. This only further continues the narrative that there is some magical aspect to a man's penis. Even as a gay man, I have found we have our own sexual scripts that we follow. I think we still prioritize the male orgasm in that tops are usually expected to orgasm (top being the man giving, bottom being the man receiving). It is intriguing because in both instances, the 'masculine' script-follower is getting rewarded."

That's the old-school script—that sex "means" a man putting his penis in a woman's vagina. Penetrative intercourse has been the norm, functioning as more or less the standard cultural definition of sex, despite its one-sidedness. There's even a slang acronym for it: PIVMO, for "penis-in-vagina-male-orgasm" sex. As one of my students says, "We can't get away from dick."

> "I love receiving oral and I have learned to be open about it and speaking up for what I want. Most guys just think penetration alone will make a girl finish and they do not engage in enough foreplay to equally pleasure the woman. I have had guys tell me before they do not even know where the clitoris is, and one guy told me that the clitoris did not exist. I literally laughed in his face and proceeded to block his number, as any girl in her right mind should."

This penetrative norm is certainly one major form of intimacy. And it's a technique that works for pregnancy, if that's your goal. But if the goal is shared pleasure in the heterosexual bed, it's best to add in other techniques as well. Give the gal a hand, with some fingering; a tongue, with some oral sex; a vibrator, with some sex toys. Ask her what feels good for her and listen closely for the words and body language of her answer.

Women's sexual pleasure is less assured in heterosexual coupling when the master narrative favors vaginal intercourse. Cliteracy instead changes the definition of sex away from penetration to whatever forms of intimacy bring mutual good feelings to the partners. Expanding this definition reduces anxiety and pressure for guys, as well. The whole notion of "erectile dysfunction" and "premature ejaculation" assumes that a man needs a hard erection for a long time to be a good lover and bring his partner to orgasm. Cliteracy teaches the simple message that he doesn't. Much unnecessary shame and deception follows from this false assumption: Women faking orgasms so the guy doesn't feel inadequate, to spare his feelings, or simply to end a session that isn't doing it for her. Guys worried they'll be judged and mocked as a "one-minute man" or a "two-pump chump." It's time for less anxiety and more enjoyment for guys, too, with freedom for them to explore wider genital pleasures (their prostate and anus, for example).

> "I've seen what some of the guys in porn look like—great bodies and massive things. I've felt like I wouldn't ever be able to perform. I've compared my own endurance to videos and felt like I wasn't really a 'man' because I couldn't last as long. It was a very self-deprecating mindset."

Cliteracy queers—it calls into question and transforms—the penis-in-vagina penetrative norm as the be-all and end-all of sex. It offers alternatives and opens a wider vision. It doesn't matter how quickly a man reaches climax in an encounter, as long as his orgasm doesn't end the action for a partner who would still like to experience her own. A man does not need his magic wand ever-erect penis to make that happen. A generous and cliterate lover knows he has other options available to him, and he's open to exploring his own wider ranging landscape of pleasure.

Cliteracy gets us beyond the convention of phallic penetration, with its limitations as a pathway to pleasure for women. It explores more diverse depictions of what gives most women more gratification: clitoral stimulation, with or without penetration, the solo joys of masturbation, and a wide range of body pleasures, all in a safe and supportive context. Everyone ends up happier all around: less shame and anxiety and faking it; more pleasure, mutuality, and making it.

Cliteracy gets us equity of pleasure.

> "It's kinda trendy to be focused on the woman orgasming in a sexual encounter now. One thing I've seen trending is that you don't lose your virginity until you've had an orgasm. I've seen a lot of TikToks recently embodying the idea the sexual encounter didn't count if you didn't finish. Hopefully more and more people will begin to get 'cliterate'!"

The orgasm gap is not only about the individual. This new wave of cliteracy has been gaining ground in various twenty-first-century conversations about what it means for society itself to become more cliterate and knowledgeable about female sexuality.

The work of conceptual artist Sophia Wallace is one trailblazing example of "artivism"—the interplay or overlap of activism (in Wallace's case, feminist activism) with art. Wallace's *Cliteracy Project*—originating in a 2012 art exhibit at a New York gallery and now encompassing a documentary film and ongoing mixed-media installations—features one hundred "natural laws" or truths and aphorisms about the clitoris and, more broadly, about the cultural illiteracy around women's sexuality. These natural laws include:

- No Justice, No Peace, No Orgasm, No Liberty.
- Penetration with a penis is just one of innumerable ways to have sex.
- Democracy without Cliteracy? Phallusy.
- 99% of porn is a monocrop of rapid penetration gratuitous ejaculation 1% plot and 0% cliteracy.
- The world isn't flat and women don't orgasm from their vaginas.

Artist Sophia Wallace standing next to her sculpture *Adamas* (Unconquerable).
Photograph courtesy of the artist, 2018.

"We are taught early on what a penis looks like. We see drawings of penises all over the place, but no one draws the clitoris. No one knows what it looks like! Why are we not more open about female pleasure as a society? Why are we so scared of the clitoris?"

"Honestly, if I did not know what these sculptures were, I probably would have guessed they were something else, and that's coming from a female who has a clit. So, yes, cliteracy should become more of a topic for everyone!"

Wallace frames cliteracy as a way to address head-on a pernicious cultural blind spot: the paradox of "the global obsession with sexualizing female bodies in a world that is maddeningly illiterate when it comes to female sexuality." Through her art, Wallace's goal is to correct ongoing misconceptions about sexuality, expose media misrepresentation, highlight the horrors of female genital mutilation, create open dialogue, and celebrate the right to human thriving and creativity for everyone.

One of Wallace's most intriguing "natural laws of cliteracy" is the claim that "freedom in society can be measured by the distribution of orgasms." One measure of who is most free in society is who can access the most pleasure. Those who have the freest agency to experience orgasm enjoy the fullest sexual citizenship. Other people, subject to forces that suppress their sexuality or weaponize it against them, are shut out of fullest agency and pleasure. The gender distribution of orgasms is thus an issue not simply of personal satisfaction but of human rights. It becomes one measure of the strength of civil society.

The World Health Organization estimates that female genital cutting, also referred to as female genital mutilation or FGM, has affected 200 million girls and women alive today. See the websites of the WHO and the Orchid Project.

Wallace highlights how pleasure is not just about mindless hedonism. Pleasure is a concept with sharp political implications about the distribution of power. Everyone, regardless of their gender, has an equal right to exist as a sexual citizen in society. People's right to sexual autonomy is not limited based on their gender—nor on their race, sexual orientation, or disability status.

> "My understanding of female sexual pleasure has been so stunted throughout my life. I learned about boys' wet dreams long before I learned I had a part of my body that was designed for my own pleasure. I internalized that sexual desire was somehow masculine, even though I was discovering my own desires. It's heartbreaking to think how much work I will have to do to undo all that I have internalized from society about my own body and the experiences I *should* have with it as I work to prioritize my own pleasure."

One other recent creative zone of cliteracy—a space in the culture that talks about female sexual pleasure—is woman-oriented erotica and romance fiction. This entertainment genre is equal parts controversial and massively popular. Beyond E. L. James's *Fifty Shades* series (which set records for the fastest-selling paperback ever), think Netflix's most-watched series, the 2020 adaptation *Bridgerton*; the online UK erotica and sex-education magazine *Cliterati*, launched in 2001; as well as the long-standing, billion-dollar, romance novel publishing industry itself, featuring levels of on-page erotic content from the mild and sweet to the five-pepper spicy—all story worlds supported by a huge and engaged online fan community.

Largely written and consumed by women, part of why this genre is controversial is precisely because it shows women's erotic desire and satisfaction. It *delights* in such scenes. This is a realm of tales, not simply about people falling in love, but of women experiencing the fullest sexual satisfaction while doing so. No need to fake it for these gals.

"My sex-ed class did not talk about female orgasms at all. They taught us how men experience pleasure sexually but not women. I don't even know if I knew women could have an orgasm. Because it wasn't taught. Now, that just seems crazy to me!"

As the coeditors of *The Feminist Porn Book* note, "Society's dread of women who own their desire, and use it in ways that confound expectations of proper female sexuality, persists." Or, as *New York Times* best-selling romance author Sarah MacLean puts it, "Romance gets the literacy stink-eye because of the sex bits." Stories of women wanting and getting hot sex from lovers who are invested in female climax and know how to deliver: that's an anxiety-provoking message for a culture more comfortable with male arousal and satisfaction than its female counterparts. When *Fifty Shades* came out to international blockbuster status, it got slapped with the shame label of "mommy porn."

"We should be teaching girls from a young age the appropriate terms for their body parts. It is also healthy to be teaching them that masturbation is okay and that they should not be ashamed to learn and explore how their body works and by doing this it will lead to healthy relationships down the road and the ability to have clear communication on what they want/need on their end."

While debates rage among scholars and readers about the feminist empowerment of the romance genre (and the literary quality of the books), here is a key to its progressive and radical message: in these narratives, women *like* sex. Their desire is taken as natural and normal and good. Never as shameful. This rise of more or less mainstream woman-oriented erotica destigmatizes female sexuality. The stories provide creative respite, a fun and sexy play field of fantasy, all while affirming love as a force for good in the world.

In this genre, women work out, within the realm of fiction, and make up for, through the pleasures of the text, a legacy of illiteracy around sexuality, as we slowly gain more cliteracy in our new gender and sexual revolution. The genre creates a space of sexual imagination, of solace and possibility. The space is safe but queer—transgressive, unruly, unacceptable to the literary hierarchy, and refusing to conform to traditional ideals of what a "proper lady" should read and write and how she should act in bed.

The rise of sex-positive American women rappers carries on in this tradition. In 2020, Cardi B released "WAP," a collaboration with Megan Thee Stallion. The chart-topping number-one single went on to become the most acclaimed song of the year. The title stands for "wet-ass pussy" and features samples from the song "Whores in This House." The lyrics and music video are gloriously—and controversially—slut-identified, pro-whore, and reveling in triumphant displays of female sexual desire and prowess.

Creative zones of cliteracy in the culture are making more space for women's erotic desire and gratification.

The term *cliterate* takes on further meaning in all these examples to describe a person who dares explore desires and fantasies that run contrary to traditional scripts for feminine sexual service, who dares expect full sexual citizenship for women. More broadly, a cliterate person is someone who assents to the mutuality of good sex. Someone who understands that good sex means shared pleasure. Someone who knows that sexual justice means orgasm equality and egalitarian power-with relationships where everybody gets to feel good, in ways that work for them.

> "Being a bi man who tends to go after guys more than girls, everything I know about sex is very un-heteronormative. In queer sexual encounters, each person is able to say exactly what they are into, where they draw their lines, and what they are willing to try. Since I am a queer man, my experiences with women may have been different than what they were used to because I prioritized their pleasure as well as mine."

Here is our new normal: twenty-first-century storytelling that features fresh scripts about gender, love, and sex. Where is this erotica going? A heterosexual BDSM romance like *Shades* was just the beginning. How about gay and lesbian and bisexual love stories of the boldest rainbow stripes, polyamorous erotica, singledom tales with happy-for-now endings, or asexual romance—all currently available at bookstores? Ideally, like all aspects of the Manisexto, this storytelling opens space in the culture. It leads toward a goal of equity and inclusion in support of sexual and gender diversity, toward a full range of consensual options for relationship pleasure, toward intimacy understood as always reciprocal and respectful.

It leads toward a climax, not only of sexual pleasure, but of a bold vision of love.

Chapter 22

CLIMAX

Drawing the Line toward New Visions of Love

The question, as Tina Turner famously belted out in her classic mega-hit, is *What's love got to do with it?* The Manisexto's answer? *Everything.*

Love of self and love of other, broadly understood, are foundational to the vision of positive sexuality. Power-with relationships celebrate respect and pleasure shared between partners—whether it's for one night or for a lifetime. Another way to put it? These relationships celebrate love.

> "Sex is better if you're both into it and are interested in each other. This doesn't mean you have to be in love or anything; it just means that both participants will have a much more pleasurable time if you have common interests and enjoy each other's company."

For some people, the term *love* might sound too sentimental or imply more commitment than is entailed when the relationship is a short fling. I'm not suggesting that sex always has to be flowery and forever. You don't have to be married to justify sex, but you do need this mutuality of respect and pleasure. Together, those qualities constitute a form of love. You don't have to *be* in love, but good sex is sex that is *loving*. It can be casual and still be loving. It can be anonymous and still be loving. Sex doesn't have to be a matter of swept-off-your-feet adoring passion for the intimacy to count as loving in this sense of kind, fair, and honorable.

This inclusive vision of love is the heart of the Manisexto. Love is the moral check against using others in a one-sided way. In the equally crucial form of self-love, it is the check against allowing oneself to be so used. The presence of love ensures power-with reciprocity in relationships. It ensures care of self and care of other. It is the key to good sex.

> "Sex is the highest vibration of love in this universe. Sex is the most powerful contender in the universe, as it holds the only force that can transcend time and space: love."

Cultural scripts about appropriate sexuality and gender norms inter-twine with scripts about love. To the ancient and perennial question of how to define the good life, American pop culture's resounding answer has been through the story line of romance: *Find your one true love and live happily ever after!* Traditionally, a man and a woman are directed to find each other (in an Insta-worthy meet-cute, if at all possible), match up as soul mates, fall deeply in love, and then settle down together to live out their happily ever after, adorable offspring pattering at their feet. While it's okay to sow some wild oats first (particularly for the guy), once the lovers bond, they are mated for life and only have eyes for each other. This romance story becomes the governing law for sexual behavior.

> "I came to this school bright-eyed and bushy-tailed. I wasn't sexually active and had no real relationships in high school. I thought I would meet a guy, fall in love with him, lose my virginity to him, then get a ring by spring and call it a day! In my dreams."

The narrative of romantic love is one of the most powerful scripts at work in the culture, although its dominance wasn't always the case. Prior to the late eighteenth century, marriage tended to be pragmatically based on considerations of money, power, and alliances. Through the nineteenth and twentieth centuries, however, the sentimental and passionate love-based match became the ideal in Western culture.

Ever since, American popular culture and entertainment media have ensured that people sop up this love plot through endless daily doses, starting in early childhood. The ideology of the romance story is inculcated—especially into young girls—through Disney princess movies, music lyrics, the wedding and diamond jewelry industries, Hollywood rom-coms, the romance publishing industry, and more. It is advertising's favorite emotional well. It is the heartbeat of America.

The ideology of the romance story is inculcated—especially into young girls—through cultural sources such as Disney princess movies, the wedding and diamond jewelry industries, and more.

Truly, there's nothing wrong with this traditional love model of how to live a good life—it's a great choice when it's the right fit for you. What's wrong is the cultural assumption that the model has to work for everyone: a one-size-fits-all vision of romance and relationship. When the story goes from a narrative to an imperative—that's when it turns problematic. The romance story becomes compulsory: the path to happiness requires obligatory passage through Romancelandia. Pair-bonded love gets portrayed as *the* way for a person to become happy.

Yes, such partnered romance does provide meaning and fulfillment for many people. And yes, romantic love can be a powerful force for good in life and a bedrock for family and childrearing. But, no—not for everyone as a mandated norm, not in the mythic and idealized form in which it often appears in cultural storytelling, and not when romance means male-led heterosexual couples only.

> "I love feeling another one's love, that deeper emotional connection is so fulfilling and makes you feel so safe and wanted."

When the romance story becomes an ideology force-fed by the culture, it obscures the wider diversity of ways to live a full and fulfilling life. It can colonize our emotions and hijack our own personal story lines. It can bind people into roles that don't necessarily meet their needs or nurture their individual growth. It can channel people into parenting for whom that role is not a good fit. When breakup or divorce results, it can shame people and leave them feeling like a failure, as it can for single people, as if they're all missing out on life's highest and best calling.

The ideology of romance leads young girls, in particular, to grow up thinking their main task in life is to find their soul mate, their Prince Charming, and to hold on tight. Chasing love in this way leads women to shortchange themselves and to sideline education and career ambitions. It leads people to stick too long in bad-fit or abusive relationships because they think they have to couple up, that love heals all wounds, that a bad romance is better than none at all.

> "I have seen girls stay in relationships that are extremely unhealthy and toxic because us as women tend to be in love with the idea of having someone and then we want to see the good in them. I have also seen men stay in relationships where they are often abused or taken advantage of, out of fear they will be blamed for everything."

While the love story continues to maintain its centrality, the romance script has changed. A new attitude toward relationship is unfolding in America, rooted in our moment of historic human rights gains. Love remains central to healthy intimacy, but with a newly queered openness to broader possibilities for marriage equality, for egalitarian relationship, as well as cultural endorsement for nonpartnered lifestyles.

What's emerging is a twenty-first-century understanding of love anchored in an inclusive vision of sex-positive romance that lets people love as they will.

After all, love is love.

> "Love wins forever and a million times over!"

American society is in the midst of writing these new scripts about sexuality and gender intertwined with love, romance, and relationship. In one prime example, we have changed the definition of marriage, through the 2015 Supreme Court decision that legalized same-sex marriage. That's a radically new story about who is allowed to partner up and live out their romantic love with the full legal sanction of society.

Some people worry here about the problem of the slippery slope: how much to allow and where to draw the line, before it all goes too far. In a groundbreaking essay entitled "Thinking Sex," anthropologist and theorist Gayle Rubin got people thinking about exactly this: What is permitted inside a society's "charmed circle" of laudable relationship? On what basis does society make decisions about which forms of sex and love are considered acceptable and which go too far and "cross the line"? Who has the privilege—and why—of their desire and love being sanctioned as good and natural and moral? All these questions begin to *queer* love—to question and challenge traditional norms, to get us thinking critically about power, equity, and the politics of pleasure.

Given that we have widened the charmed circle to include same-sex marriage, what's next? As we open the gates further (and, in the case of the also-prominent debate about transgender rights, open access to the bathrooms and the sports teams), what happens?

The question, for me, is not what we draw the line *against*, but what we draw the line *toward*. Instead of fear-mongering, we can engage in compassion. Instead of diatribes that society must draw its hard line in the sand against dangerous changes to the tried-and-true, we can reframe the conversation as drawing a line toward new possibilities of love. Same-sex marriage, for example, already points toward equality in options for romance partnership.

The line to be evaluated, for me, is whether the relationship intimacy upholds the principles of positive sexuality and gender equity: that sexuality is a normal, healthy, and pleasurable aspect of being human and that people have the right to their sexual choices, as long as those choices are consensual and support partners' best interests and autonomy, equally empowering and pleasurable to all. The sex-positive ethic we've developed invites the full acceptance into society's charmed circle of such consent-based sexual and gender diversity.

Another way to frame this question about where to draw the line is to say that society itself gets to consent too. The question of informed consent is not only a matter for discussion between partners in sexual encounters but is also a matter for public discussion—through the media, the enactment of new laws, the setting of workplace policies, and a million everyday conversations happening all across the country. Through the new gender and sexual revolution, society is changing what it consents to count as acceptable or ethical behavior. The #MeToo movement, for example, is drawing its own line in the sand against abuse that used to be tolerated or quietly hushed up. This change means that, going forward, society's collective task is to figure out a consensus on these updated scripts about sexuality.

It's worth remembering that for much of American history, core aspects of gender and sexuality that we now deem acceptable used to be widely vilified as sinful and wrong. In various examples, what was once viewed as illicit, illegal, immoral, impossible is now uncontroversial and accepted, pretty much across the political spectrum. These examples include birth control for married couples, divorce, women's voting rights, and interracial marriage. On all these points, impassioned historical debate argued for society's downfall should the change be allowed. The change happened, and we judge ourselves better off and more enfranchised with stronger civil rights because of it.

Today's expansion zones of the charmed circle include two frontiers in particular. The consent of society is starting to move these two new developments into mainstream ascendance, along with a set of terms used and heard more often as they enter everyday language.

First, society is increasingly thinking outside the couple norm, on a variety of fronts. A growing singledom movement supports singletons who craft their own happy endings in serial relationships (a lifetime of shorter couplings, instead of the grand one-true-love couple ideal) or through a found-family circle of friends (cultivating the love of friendship itself as an equally appealing alternative to the romantic couple norm). Others practice polyamory: consensual nonmonogamy or open relationships, where people have two or more partners at the same time (throuples instead of couples, as well as quads and moresomes),

Check out the website of International Pronouns Day, now marked in October every year. As their website states, "International Pronouns Day seeks to make respecting, sharing and educating about personal pronouns commonplace. Referring to people by the pronouns they determine for themselves is basic to human dignity. Being referred to by the wrong pronouns particularly affects transgender and gender nonconforming people. Together, we can transform society to celebrate people's multiple, intersecting identities."

not cheating or hiding an affair, but with everyone's open knowledge and consent. The critique of couple-normativity also aligns with the asexuality movement. People who are asexual or aromantic pose a viable alternative to the couple norm. The best relationship may be with yourself; no one *needs* a boyfriend, girlfriend, or love partner to be complete.

A second new development moving into the mainstream is that many people now list their preferred pronouns and some people have adopted the singular use of they/them pronouns. These practices were acknowledged by the American Dialect Society with their vote for "(my) pronouns" as the 2019 "Word of the Year," a selection they said "speaks to how the personal expression of gender identity has become an increasing part of our shared discourse." International Pronouns Day, established in 2018, is recognized around the world. Many people choose to list the pronouns they use in their email signatures, social media profiles, or when they're introduced ("Hi, my name is Catherine, and I use she/her pronouns"). The move is related to the rise of people who identify as gender queer or gender-nonconforming and who live contentedly outside the male-female binary.

> "I one hundred percent believe that we are moving away from a strict gender binary. We should allow people to find comfort in whatever gender expression feels authentic for them."

Two hundred years ago, our nineteenth-century ancestors would have struggled to imagine interracial or same-sex unions celebrated in marriage ceremonies that are officially sanctioned by state and church. But here we are! It's equally difficult for folk today to imagine what our descendants' lives might look like, two hundred years from now. Given this history of cultural change, important values to help us through the current moment include humility and openness to the future, in order to imagine ourselves into an ever-freer world.

AFTERGLOW

Where We Go from Here

Toward Better Sex Education in America

If you want big, bold ideas about how to "make America great" (again or ever), here's my recommendation: try better sex ed.

Sex education is the call to action that follows as the necessary conclusion of the Manisexto's five commitments to positive sexuality, the normalization of diversity, body acceptance, consent, and shared pleasure. Good sex—in the dual sense we've been using of *good* as both ethical and enjoyable—requires good sex ed.

To illustrate the point, I offer this longer story from one of my students. The story helps give a sense of the ongoing barriers to high-quality sex education and these barriers' roots in America's complex history of ambivalence toward sexuality.

Jake (not his actual name) is a white guy in his mid-twenties; he's a few years older than traditional college age, as he took time off to work before returning to school to complete his education. He's majoring in psychology, already doing an internship in counseling, and, from the beginning of term, engages enthusiastically with the course material. I'd asked all the students to write their first reflection paper on the sex education they received growing up, whether it followed a curriculum that was "abstinence-only" or a more comprehensive approach to sexuality, and how they now evaluate the quality and impact of that sex ed experience looking back. This is what Jake wrote:

> So, abstinence versus comprehensive sex education. This is a pretty easy decision for me. I was raised in Alabama and had almost zero sex education. In 9th or 10th grade, the entire class was gathered in the auditorium for a few hours one day, and we were shown a bunch of pictures of STD-infected genitalia and other body parts. Like gonorrhea in someone's eyeball. That one will always stick with me. Then, in health class, we watched a video. All I can remember is that male ejaculate comes out at 27 miles per hour and very graphic images of some lady giving birth.
>
> At the end of all this, we had to sign some abstinence pledge, which of course I did, because as a fourteen- or fifteen-year-old I was terrified. For like a day or two. I, of course, had sex the first opportunity that came my way. Like the statistics show, we did not use protection, because what's the point if we'd been taught it doesn't work anyway?
>
> I certainly wish I had been given more useful knowledge and I would guess that most kids would say the same.

For many people, the conclusion is obvious: we need better and more comprehensive sex education. Jake's story—not at all uncommon—provides strong grounds for the argument that school systems should provide high-quality sexuality and relationship education to all young people. If you need further convincing, here's a disturbing statistic to add to Jake's account: almost half of all pregnancies in America are unplanned.

Throughout my years of teaching the Sexuality & Society course, I've heard endless versions of Jake's story from the students. Many of these young people, looking back, say their sex ed was horrible. Like, really horrible. Along the lines of *Mean Girls* horrible, where the gym coach teaches sex ed with the lesson, "Don't have sex, because you will get pregnant and die!" Students laugh ruefully about that movie quote as spot-on to their school experience. They remember being taught to "just keep your knees together" and advised to avoid infections by "staying away from nasty people."

"As young people, we have the right to make informed decisions without feeling ashamed of talking about sex. Sex education should be just as much of a right as the freedom of speech and expression."

The girls' lessons—classes are often split up by gender, unlike any other academic subject, as if people of all genders don't need to learn about menstruation or unintended erections—are full of the worst fear- and shame-based messaging imaginable. Women students tell me about classes where they had to pass around a rose, plucking off one petal at a time; the teacher told them the thorny stem at the end would be them if they had sex with multiple boys. Or the piece

According to the American Guttmacher Center for Population Research Innovation and Dissemination, 45 percent or *almost half* of all pregnancies in the US are unintended, a higher rate than in many other developed countries.

of tape put on and peeled off each girl's arm in turn, until it couldn't stick to anyone: "That would be you, no longer able to form an attachment, if you sleep around like a slut." Or the paper cup, passed around, everybody directed to spit into it in turn, and then the question at the end: "Who wants to drink from *that*?" My heart breaks for them all.

"The scary part pertaining to sex ed is that intimacy is a major part of our lives, like driving. We require driving school and driving tests. Most students open a bank account when they get their first job and are taught about money management. But how are the lessons about intimacy, identity, and gender taught to young adults? They typically aren't, so when students turn to porn and dramatized media outlets, they are getting a version that is not real. It's like if an actor on television races a car and tells young people this is the best way to drive."

While some lucky students considered their sex ed to be positive, most thought their school experience was lacking and that it should have done more. Many felt badly let down by their teachers and more or less abandoned to figure things out on their own. Porn, peers, and the internet became their default sources of learning about how to deal with their changing bodies and burgeoning sexuality. One of the most consistent messages I hear from my students, over and over, is that America needs better and more comprehensive sex education nationwide for its young people.

"The day I learned about how my body works in
sex education, Dad picked me up from school and
I could not shut up about it. I guess I made him
uncomfortable, and he told Mom about the awkward car
ride. Mom yelled at him to go back in there, be excited
with me, and take the information like a champ! She was
so upset that he would not listen to what I learned about
myself that day. The story still gets brought up in our family
as something to laugh about because he was stuck in a
household with all girls."

Parents, of course, make a huge difference. They can make up for lacks in the school system. Often, however, what holds both parents and educators back is that we're too scared and embarrassed, too insecure and uninformed ourselves—because of these repeated cycles of miseducation—to offer any real help. Ideally, parents and schools work together to break these cycles and get over this discomfort. Ideally, sex education involves young people, parents, schools, educators, and health-care professionals in promoting honest and transparent discussion.

"My mother never talked to me about sex, and when
I asked why she said she figured I learned from other
kids. I was honestly confused, 'So you are okay with
me learning about an intimate topic like sex from other
kids?' She had no reply, but then I realized my mom could
not talk to me about sex because no one ever talked to her
about it. I think it is almost a generational curse to not be
educated on something we all will eventually do."

Of all areas of public policy, sexuality education is the most neglected. Because of the legacy of American ambivalence toward sex that we traced in chapter 4, sex itself remains a taboo topic. Sex education is politically charged and underrepresented even within progressive or liberal policy platforms. In no other area of policy or education do we tolerate such deliberate withholding of information necessary to personal well-being. Global organizations such as the United Nations and World Health Organization view sex ed as a human right entrenched by international treaties. Only twenty-nine US states, however, mandate sex education; even worse, only eleven require lessons on consent. According to a Centers for Disease Control and Prevention (CDC) study conducted in 2018, only 43 percent of high schools and 18 percent of middle schools teach all sixteen key topics recommended by the CDC.

This neglect must end.

Not only do American youth *want* better sex education, they badly need it. The overwhelming sense I get from my years of working with young people is how much trauma they endure around issues of gender, the body, and intimate relationships. Across the entire spectrum of gender and sexual identity, this trauma is pervasive. It's hard to grow up in America without suffering some form of harm in regard to your body image, your gender, your sexuality. It begins with children who

#GenerationEquality. In 2021, the UN published a global status report on comprehensive sexuality education, which it views as key to gender equality. The report documents important worldwide progress and the need for further educational efforts. See *The Journey towards Comprehensive Sexuality Education*. See also the UN's newly launched "Generation Equality" campaign, with focus on sexuality education.

are policed and shamed into societal roles that never fit absolutely. It continues with young adults whose sexual consent is routinely violated, often without them fully understanding they should have a choice. The shameful and tragic failure of sex ed instruction leaves young people underprepared for a high-stakes area of life. Those headed to college arrive unequipped for leading responsible and pleasurable sex lives. With guys pressured by toxic masculinity, girls trained to please, and alcohol fueling a party environment, it's little wonder that campuses end up with some of the highest rates of sexual violence.

Better sex education would not completely eliminate all these forms of trauma, but it could go very far to alleviate it.

We need comprehensive sex ed, now.

"There's a big danger in avoiding discussions about sex. Young people are forced to figure a lot of stuff out on their own and this leads to problems. The more educated individuals are, the closer we will be to ending sexual harassment."

Everyone needs opportunities to learn how to make informed decisions consistent with their values and in support of their well-being regarding consensual relationships—whether those relationships be virginal, asexual, celibate, heterosexual, gay, lesbian, bisexual, queer, transgender, or any other hue of the rainbow. Young people especially need information that is medically accurate and shame-free. There are basic things everyone needs to know about how bodies work in order to stay healthy and to feel good about their bodies. These basics about reproductive health care— sexual anatomy, human reproduction, how to avoid unwanted pregnancy and sexually transmitted infections or diseases (STIs or STDs)—are only the beginning. Such lessons can be taught repeatedly, in age-appropriate and engaging ways, throughout the settings of primary, middle, and high schools, so that young people can learn to ensure their well-being and that of their partners. Comprehensive sex ed, however, isn't only about the menstrual cycle or how to use a condom.

"Nobody would stand for a country's education system not including instruction in mathematics, and so why do we think it is okay to not include sex ed? Sexuality is a basic part of life, so why would any nation intentionally allow for entire generations of individuals to be ignorant of the most basic science behind the subject?"

A full curriculum encompasses much more—including open discussion about how *not* everyone needs to have sex or have kids, if that's not their choice. It eliminates the coercive cultural pressure to be sexually active (virgin- and prude-shaming), romantically paired up (couple-normativity), and the slut-shaming if one is deemed *too* active. The approach of a comprehensive curriculum is trauma-informed and justice-oriented. It embraces gender equity by teaching an inclusive feminist message about equality in intimate relationships, empowered gender roles in society, and options for masculinity lived outside the Man Box. It is queer-friendly in centering and affirming kids both queer and straight. It imparts self-advocacy skills. A robust curriculum includes lessons on good communication and responsible decision-making, on being *really* clear about mutual consent, and on the impact of media and pornography. At its core, it teaches people to honor their desire, their self, and their partners. It embodies the fundamental message that sex is good—is better, more pleasurable, and more ethical—when you know you're acting in line with the desires, values, best interests, and boundaries of yourself and any partners.

Decades of research on successful models of education confirm the value of this approach to developing a healthy gender and sexual self-image. Such gender and sexual literacy is as important as reading literacy, computer literacy, and math lit-

Check out these education models for supporting healthy sexual citizenship and sexually healthy communities:

• Our Whole Lives (OWL) Lifespan Sexuality Education
• Dr. Amy Schalet's ABCD (autonomy, building healthy relationships, connectedness, diversity) model
• Centers for Disease Control and Prevention, *Adolescent Health: What Works in Schools*
• The United Nations, *International Technical Guidance on Sexuality Education: An Evidence-Informed Approach*, revised edition
• AMAZE, using the power of digital media to work with partners around the globe

eracy—all standard components of kids' education. Research confirms as well the failure—and expense—of public health approaches that teach only abstinence. Journalist Peggy Orenstein concluded that the $1.7 billion in federal funding for abstinence-only education "might just as well have been set on fire." So-called "purity culture" in the 1980s (with an emphasis on teen pledges to save sex for marriage) led to abstinence-only sex education programs financed by the US government. Evangelical Christian organizations promoted these programs along with a view of sex as shameful and dangerous unless within marriage, itself conceived as a heterosexual and male-led norm of family life for everyone. Problem is, long-term studies prove these programs don't stop young people from having sex. They do, however, result in higher rates of teen pregnancy and can cause lasting damage.

> "After a lifetime of indoctrination, feelings of dirtiness and sinfulness do not automatically dissipate after vows are exchanged. I know newlyweds who struggle with communication regarding intimacy and young women burdened with vaginismus and irreparable feelings of shame and guilt as a result of purity culture."

In contrast, the potential impact of comprehensive sex education—offered in kindergarten through high school, in colleges and universities, and in public health settings across communities—is surprisingly wide. It's particularly crucial for marginalized and vulnerable communities—such as queer youth, people who are disabled, and people of color—who already suffer health disparities. But such knowledge is for everyone, at all stages of life, so we can function well as human beings and thrive in our relationships.

Good sex ed supports the personal well-being and cultural competence of individuals, at the same time that it supports the flourishing of society. Besides teaching about healthy intimate relationships, high-quality sexuality and relationship education helps at a societal level to end cycles of poverty, address child abuse, empower girls and women, provide alternatives to toxic masculinity (with its documented ill effects on boys' and men's health), reduce domestic violence and sexual assault, cut workplace harassment and improve productivity, promote racial equality, lessen transphobia and homophobia, foster diversity and inclusion, and generally help America achieve its core commitment to justice.

Yes—good sex ed *can* do all that. We can absolutely achieve transformative cultural change through comprehensive sex education. #SexEdSavesLives

There is no downside to a robust curriculum of relationship and sexuality education. For the leery who worry it grants license for hormonal teens to open the floodgates to immorality, remember that, contrary to misinterpretation, a positive sexuality approach does *not* teach "anything goes." Through lessons about informed consent, this approach insists on a strict moral responsibility framework of sexual ethics, with emphasis on accountability and respect for self and others. Its discussion of desire and pleasure is never about one-sided and self-indulgent gratification. Not all sex is okay. The consideration is always for partnered sex to be egalitarian, mutual, shared, and reciprocal. Pleasure is not dangerous hedonism when one values the satisfaction of a partner's desire as much as one's own. Positive sexuality is always ethical sexuality.

My university has a slogan: *This is how college is meant to be*. Sometimes my colleagues and I are cynical about it: *You mean college is all about swanky dorms and tricked-out rec centers, endless frat parties and football mania?* But working with young people in the Sexuality & Society course has taught me how the slogan is inspiring as well, in that it upholds the mission of the university—not just my school, but any institution of higher learning. College *is* meant to be a time and place of critical inquiry, of innovation and discovery. As I've said, teachers and students are meant to query and queer everything, to push incessantly forward the boundaries of new knowledge. This educational enterprise is an act of hope for a better world. It is, in essence, an act of love.

Education around positive sexuality enacts exactly that hope: the hope that we can craft a better, more just, and more loving world. The commitment to better sex education is key to realizing the potential of the cultural change we've traced in this book. Within the last decade, same-sex marriage became legal, the #MeToo movement exploded, colleges nationwide came to teach consent-based sexual health, the media learned to celebrate body positivity, and transgender visibility went mainstream. Our present-day moment of gender and sexual revolution is getting American society closer to good sex: sex that is both good, as in ethical, and good, as in pleasurable. This moment—supported by forthright sex education—promises a pivotal turning point in the quest toward social justice.

"With all topics of sexuality, I believe the steps in the right direction for our society always start with education, to lead to more understanding and acceptance and to create a brighter and better future for everyone."

None of this is to deny the harsh realities of backlash. This moment of hope exposes ongoing pain. While there have been historic gains in legal protection and changed attitudes, divisive politics call these gains into question daily. Many people are *not* experiencing a consistent flourishing of their rights and freedoms. Instead, they experience renewed vulnerability to an angry minority who view this cultural shift as a provocation and take it as reason for hostility. The Human Rights Campaign reports that in 2021 twenty-five anti-LGBTQ bills were enacted into law in state legislatures around the country and that it was the deadliest year on record for transgender and gender nonconforming people in the US. These incidences of fatal violence disproportionately affect people of color. Such violent pushback can make claims of progress seem delusional, a form of toxic positivity. Progress may seem like a false hope only able to bloom because it comes from a place of privilege sheltered from such violence—a cruel hope for those not seeing the fruits of this change.

The key is that this transformational shift is largely one of *generational* shift. Here is the source for the hope. The rapid changes in the sex/gender landscape are led by the younger generation. Youth are the vanguard, blazing new trails into this landscape and marking out a new common ground. As noted, this Gen Z demographic provides the clearest window on America at the tipping point, with their 84 percent support for marriage equality and one in six identifying as LGBT.

> "In the United States, adults love to talk about the future in terms of career goals and milestones and love to give us advice. Adults constantly look for opportunities to teach youth, but there is one topic that is left in the dark, and that is sex."

I hear this message consistently from my students (after they agree on the need for better sex ed): they're fine with these new norms of diversity and inclusion. They are themselves—or they know people who are—gay, lesbian, bisexual, pansexual, polyamorous, gender nonconforming, nonbinary, trans, queer, and out in all sorts of ways. At a minimum, they experience such diversity as more visible and mainstream than did their parents' generation. Nowadays, diversity is just *there*. Young people are less bewildered or threatened by it. They see a commitment to diversity as offering more freedom for people to live in authentic ways and more accountability—less sweeping under the rug—when people try to oppress others and abuse power.

Another way to put this point about social change and hope is that it's not the liberal left on college campuses who are indoctrinating young people into a radical political agenda, as one sometimes hears. Young people, more open-minded and less entrenched in power structures than their elders, are leading the way themselves. *They* are the social progressives driving this transformational cultural shift. Working with young people provides endless hope because of their courage, despite their stories of trauma, to believe in a better future.

There is certainly a risk to be avoided here of magical thinking. Positive change is not preordained. It won't happen without activism and vigilance. But it is aided by flipping the script away from bad sex and toward imagining ourselves into the future we hope to inhabit. Hope itself becomes an activist tool for change.

> "Sex oftentimes gets a bad rap. We are told to be afraid of it until marriage, and we often only learn of how things can go wrong. Sex is not a bad thing, and you deserve good sex with a partner who cares about you and respects you."

It's a lesson I learned from the students. They are not eager to spend a whole term talking about rape. The discussion feels scary and depressing, it triggers anxiety and memories of trauma, and it can demonize males as potential rapists while obscuring the extent to which they are victims as well. The focus drives people away from an important conversation. Instead, students respond much more enthusiastically, with greater critical engagement, when I ask them to think through meanings and pathways of good sex.

The goal, after all, is not only to *decrease* sexual wrongdoing and misconduct but also to *increase* sexual right-doing and good conduct. When we flip the script away from bad sex, we get to focus on the hope-filled and much more enjoyable task of imagining, in its fullest, *what good sex looks like*. The answer is that healthy sexuality affirms desire and, with it, self-respect and respect for partners.

The task becomes to think through the complexities of sex and imagine our way into a better future, a more sex-positive world. Not in the sense of a world with *more* sex, but bolder and more authentic sex. Sex based on people's choice, not coercion or tired cultural scripts written from old hierarchies and exclusions. Sex that is hot and consensual. Sex that eschews shame and guilt and toxic double standards. Sex that revels in pleasure for everyone. Sex that celebrates sexuality as a pathway for self-discovery, creativity, and connection.

In this better world, we define sexual justice not simply as an absence—no law breaking or violation of ethics—but as a presence, a fullness. A world where all young people get to grow into a healthy sense of their sexual agency. A democracy with equal opportunity for all to exercise their sexual citizenship, to access and share intimacy in line with their desire. An equity of pleasure that supports orgasm equality. We end up flipping the script about sex away from power-over and toward power-with. Away from fear and toward joy.

This book has been an experiment in hope, an attempt to have a positive impact on the American culture wars around sexuality by charting out the good in the new landscape. The tone is deliberately optimistic, to harness the power of imagining this better world. What results is a manifesto that affirms the justice of positive sexuality, equity for marginalized people, confident body image, informed adult consent, and lusty yet responsible pleasure, all supported through high-quality sex education.

Good Sex provides the grounds for hope that America's intertwined history of racial, sexual, and gender injustice can be resolved. The new gender and sexual revolution is strengthening civil society and freedom, in line with a quintessentially American declaration about people's right to pursue happiness and love.

We end up, then, at this vision of inclusion.

A vision that has diversity as its pulsing heart and a loving community basking in its glow.

A vision that has care and respect as its ethos and pleasure as its breathless climax.

A vision that is good, leading us forward.

ACKNOWLEDGMENTS AND NOTE ON STUDENT RESPONSES

My first acknowledgment and debt of gratitude goes to my undergraduate students at the University of Alabama. This book came into being because of them and would not have been possible without them.

For well over twenty years, I've taught at this large state university in the leafy college town of Tuscaloosa and published research on how gender, sexuality, and love play out in various corners of American pop culture, from strip clubs to romance novels. In my courses, I actively encourage registration by students of all genders and sexual orientations and seek to run my classroom as an open and affirming safe space of critical inquiry. Our public university attracts a predominantly white student body and has one of the biggest "Greek" systems of sororities and fraternities. It also has a significant population of students of color, international students, ROTC trainees and military veterans, and first-generation students. I've been teaching these collegians sexuality and gender studies, first in a small departmental seminar and then also in a much larger cross-university lecture course entitled Sexuality & Society, scaled up in size and offered every term out of a sense of mission I felt that I needed to do more to create a campus-wide curricular space for discussion and learning.

The cross-university course has proven very popular. Sexuality & Society has now enrolled hundreds of students majoring in a broad range of programs—engineering to religious studies, public relations to math. They're all young but otherwise very diverse, hailing from a mix of racial, ethnic, religious, and socioeconomic backgrounds. More than half come to Alabama from states all over the country, and the course attracts a significant number of international students, from South America to Saudi Arabia and beyond. As the students file into the lecture hall on the first day, I ask them to complete a survey about why they're taking the course. Overwhelmingly, they write about wanting to increase their understanding about sexuality. Stories and imagery about sex are everywhere in the culture, yet sex is still confusingly taboo to talk about in any sort of open way. The students are trying to figure out relationships, desire, and pleasure in their personal lives and issues of diversity, equity, and inclusion in their communities and the workplace. As new adults, it's a whole lot to manage.

The students, I discovered, are very eager for a classroom setting that allows for real discussion. They want to know: how can sex be good and be for the good? They want resources that will equip them to make healthy decisions and feel competent to handle complexity and change around gender and sexuality in society—a learning opportunity that allows them to think, read, study, and write.

They write *a lot*. Astute, insightful, moving first-person accounts about this present-day moment of change in America. Although I never ask for or require the students to share personal stories, they often do. Many of their stories haunt me and lead me to connect some of the students with campus counseling and support services. In this context, my motivation to write the book is harm reduction: to work with these courageous students toward a future of less ignorance, trauma, and hate and more knowledge, justice, and love. The stories are not all negative, as many students discover community, empowerment, and a greater sense of self and purpose among the joys of college. For some, hookup culture delivers on its seductive promise of sexual liberation. Some find friends similar to themselves, whereas before they felt alone and isolated in their sexual or gender identity. Two people even met as classmates in my course, fell in love, and went on to get married—my first student wedding.

It is these young people you hear from in the book, through their written work for my courses. All responses are presented anonymously from students who voluntarily signed up to participate in this project and who granted me written informed consent for permission to quote from their coursework in the book. I draw the quotes from the students' regular weekly writing assignments on our course material—readings, lectures, documentaries, guest speakers, and class discussions. I present the excerpts verbatim, although corrected as needed for spelling and grammar (I *am* a professor). Some of the student quotes are lightly edited for clarity and length. In a few cases, I change certain personal details to further protect student privacy. I thank, deeply, all of these students for their willingness to engage with our course ideas and this book project. I am equally grateful to a series of brilliant New College teaching assistants who helped me run the Sexuality & Society course and without whom I would have been lost.

In other debts of gratitude, I thank my husband, Ted Trost. I could say it's for all the good sex throughout the years—and I wouldn't be lying—but it's also because he's the one who came up with the term *manisexto*. One of the man's specialties in life is goofy puns. He makes them up like an oak tree sheds acorns in the fall; at the slightest breeze, the words come a-tumblin'. One day when I was muttering about a book I wanted to write, something like a manifesto about sexuality, he turned to me and said, "You mean a *manisexto*?"

Many other people generously contributed to the project, whether with publishing opportunities and advice, input from their areas of academic expertise, assistance with editing and structural development, or encouragement as I struggled with the project. I thank all these colleagues and friends for the invaluable help of their kind interest and astute critical feedback: Courtney Miller-Callihan, George Thompson, Hsu-Ming Teo, Natalie Adams, Clarissa Smith, Mark McCormick, Paige McCormick, Ann Brooks, Hannah McCann, Suzanne Younger, Lisa Dorr, Marie Metelnick, Charlotte Petonic, Jonathan Allan, Natalie Stoljar, Eric Selinger, Lane McLelland, Julia Cherry, Kathy Trost, Barbara Brickman, Ashley Runyon, the Goddess Cocktail Collective, the team of ever-excellent professionals at Indiana University Press, a series of anonymous peer reviewers, and others I fear I'm forgetting. My appreciation to you all!

For various forms of support and engagement during earlier and later stages of the book's development, I gratefully acknowledge New College, the Dean's Office of the College of Arts & Sciences, the Mallet Honors Assembly, the Research Grants Committee, Safe Zone, the Alabama Alliance for Sexual and Reproductive Justice, and the Department of Gender & Race Studies, all at the University of Alabama. For hosting research presentations or writing residencies, I thank New College of Florida; the University of Roehampton, UK; Aristotle University of Thessaloniki, Greece, and the Greek Fulbright Commission; the European University Institute, Florence, Italy; Flinders University, Adelaide, Australia; the Muriel Gold Senior Visiting Professorship at the Institute for Gender, Sexuality, & Feminist Studies at McGill University in Montreal, Canada; and the Institute for Advanced Studies in the Humanities at the University of Edinburgh.

SOURCE CITATIONS AND RESOURCES FOR FURTHER READING

Foreplay: Introducing the Mani*sexto*

p. 1 Then vice president Joe Biden endorsed transgender rights as a crucial civil rights issue: Emily Wax-Thibodeaux, "Biden's Ambitious LGBT Agenda Poises Him to Be Nation's Most Pro-equality President in History," *Washington Post*, Jan. 11, 2021, www.washingtonpost.com/politics/2021/01/11/biden-lgbtq-policies/.

p. 1 The percentage of married households in the US hit a historic low: Sally Curtin and Paul Sutton, "Marriage Rates in the United States, 1900–2018," National Center for Health Statistics, 2020, www.cdc.gov/nchs/data/hestat/marriage_rate_2018/marriage_rate_2018.htm.

p. 2 "The decision is the strongest evidence yet": Adam Nagourney and Jeremy W. Peters, "A 6-to-3 Decision Few Expected," *New York Times*, June 16, 2020, 1.

p. 4 As of 2022, marriage equality for same-sex couples exists in thirty-one countries: Human Rights Campaign Foundation, "Marriage Equality Around the World," www.hrc.org/resources/marriage-equality-around-the-world; Council on Foreign Relations, "Marriage Equality: Global Comparisons," www.cfr.org/backgrounder/marriage-equality-global-comparisons.

p. 5 Peggy Orenstein, *Girls & Sex: Navigating the Complicated New Landscape* (New York: Harper, 2016) and *Boys & Sex: Young Men on Hookups, Love, Porn, Consent, and Navigating the New Masculinity* (New York: Harper, 2020).

p. 6 "The world is indeed at a moment of Gender Vertigo": Barbara Risman, *Where the Millennials Will Take Us: A New Generation Wrestles with the Gender Structure* (New York: Oxford University Press, 2018), 305.

p. 6 "We have arrived at a pivotal moment with regard to rape culture": Donna Freitas, *Consent on Campus: A Manifesto* (New York: Oxford University Press, 2018), 7.

p. 6 In 2014, the California state legislature enacted a legal standard: Reid Wilson, "California to Require 'Affirmative Consent' before Sex," *Washington Post*, Sept. 29, 2014, www.washingtonpost.com/blogs/govbeat/wp/2014/09/29/california-to-require-affirmative-consent-before-sex/. See also Nick Anderson and Peyton Craighill, "College Students Remain Deeply Divided over What Consent Actually Means," *Washington Post*, June 14, 2015, www.washingtonpost.com/local/education/americas-students-are-deeply-divided-on-the-meaning-of-consent-during-sex/2015/06/11/bbd303e0-04ba-11e5-a428-c984eb077d4e_story.html.

p. 8 Here in Alabama, a pair of opposing rallies took place: Josh Moon, "Ray Moore Protest Attracts Variety of Views," *Montgomery Advertiser*, Jan. 12, 2016, www.montgomeryadvertiser.com/story/news/local/blogs/moonblog/2016/01/12/roy-moore-protest-attracts-opposition-oddities/78707922/.

p. 8 "According to a 2019 study": Cassie Miller and Rachel Carroll Rivas, *The Year in Hate and Extremism 2021*, Southern Poverty Law Center, March 9, 2022, www.splcenter.org/20220309/year-hate-extremism-2021.

p. 8 Risman, in her sociological study, asks: Risman, *Where the Millennials Will Take Us*, 1, 2.

p. 9 As feminist icon Gloria Steinem said: "Gloria Steinem Is Nowhere Near Done with Being an Activist," *New York Times Magazine*, Sept. 13, 2020, 14.

Manisexto #1: Positive Sexuality

p. 16 Scarleteen: sex ed for the real world. Heather Corinna, "Sexuality: WTF Is It, Anyway?" www.scarleteen.com/article/bodies/sexuality_wtf_is_it_anyway.

p. 16 American artist Sophia Wallace makes the claim: Sophia Wallace, *Cliteracy: 100 Natural Laws*, 2012, www.sophiawallace.com/cliteracy-100-natural-laws.

p. 17 Carole S. Vance, ed., *Pleasure and Danger: Exploring Female Sexuality* (Boston: Routledge & Kegan Paul, 1984).

p. 27 I am not saying that sex has to be reproductive. For further reading on alternatives and critiques to the heterosexual reproductive imperative, see, for example: Amy Agigian, *Baby Steps: How Lesbian Alternative Insemination Is Changing the World* (Middletown, CT: Wesleyan University Press, 2004); Catriona Mortimer-Sandilands and Bruce Erickson, eds., *Queer Ecologies: Sex, Nature, Politics, Desire* (Bloomington: Indiana University Press, 2010).

p. 31 Sex educator Dr. Emily Nagoski describes it: Emily Nagoski, "Sex Positive," *The Dirty Normal: Better Sex, Powered by Science*, June 27, 2010, https://thedirtynormal.com/post/2010/06/27/sex-positive/. See also her book *Come As You Are: The Surprising New Science That Will Transform Your Sex Life*, revised ed. (New York: Simon & Schuster, 2021).

p. 32 Eva Illouz, an international scholar on emotions and communication: Eva Illouz, *Hard-Core Romance:* Fifty Shades of Grey, *Best-sellers, and Society* (Chicago: University of Chicago Press, 2014), 7.

p. 32 Acceptance of same-sex marriage continues to grow: Justin McCarthy, "U.S. Support for Gay Marriage Stable, at 63%" Gallup, May 22, 2019, https://news.gallup.com/poll/257705/support-gay-marriage-stable.aspx.

p. 33 *GGG*: A nice bit of sex-positive urban lingo: Dan Savage, "SL Letter of the Day: The Limits of GGG," *Savage Love*, March 7, 2012, www.thestranger.com/slog/archives/2012/03/07/sl-letter-of-the-day-the-limits-of-ggg.

p. 38 They developed an influential theory: William Simon and John H. Gagnon, *Sexual Conduct: The Social Sources of Human Sexuality*, 2nd ed. (New York: Routledge, 2017). See also Simon and Gagnon, "Sexual Scripts: Origins, Influences and Changes," *Qualitative Sociology* 26, no. 4 (2003): 491–7.

p. 38 For further reading about sexuality in world religions, see, for example, Dag Oistein Endsjo, *Sex and Religion: Teachings and Taboos in the History of World Faiths*, translated by Peter Graves (London: Reaktion Books, 2011).

p. 39 For some sources on the history of sex in America, see, for example, Peter Gardella, *Innocent Ecstasy: How Christianity Gave America an Ethic of Sexual Pleasure* (Oxford: Oxford University Press, 1985); Tracy Fessenden et al., eds., *The Puritan Origins of American Sex: Religion, Sexuality, and National Identity in American Literature* (London: Routledge, 2001); Richard Godbeer, *Sexual Revolution in Early America* (Baltimore: Johns Hopkins University Press, 2002); Jone Johnson Lewis, "Free Love and Women's History," ThoughtCo, July 31, 2021, https://www.thoughtco.com/free-love-and-womens-history-3530392.

p. 42 For further information and documents about John Humphrey Noyes and the Oneida community, see the online "Oneida Community Collection," Syracuse University Libraries, https://library.syr.edu/scrc/collections/digitalasset/oneida.php.

p. 49 For further reading about intersectionality and intersectional feminism, see, for example, Kimberlé Crenshaw, *On Intersectionality: Essential Writings* (New York: The New Press, 2022); Patricia Hill Collins and Sirma Bilge, *Intersectionality*, 2nd ed. (Cambridge, UK: Polity Press, 2020); Brittney Cooper, *Eloquent Rage: A Black Feminist Discovers Her Superpower* (New York: St. Martin's Press, 2018).

Manisexto #2: Equity and Inclusion

p. 58 National Education Association, Just and Equitable Schools project, www
.nea.org/professional-excellence/just-equitable-schools.

p. 60 United Nations campaign, "Free and Equal," www.unfe.org/intersex
-awareness/.

pp. 60–61 As sociologist Barbara Risman notes: Barbara Risman, *Where the Millennials Will Take Us: A New Generation Wrestles with the Gender Structure* (New York: Oxford University Press, 2018), 63.

p. 61 United States National Institutes of Health, Sexual and Gender Minority Research Office, https://dpcpsi.nih.gov/sgmro.

p. 61 Generation Z young adults . . . are leading the way: Jeffrey M. Jones, "LGBT Identification Rises to 5.6% in Latest U.S. Estimate," Gallup, Feb. 24, 2021, https://news.gallup.com/poll/329708/lgbt-identification-rises-latest
-estimate.aspx. See also Christina Morales, "More Adult Americans Are Identifying as L.G.B.T., Gallup Poll Finds," *New York Times*, Feb. 24, 2021, www.nytimes.com/2021/02/24/us/lgbt-identification-usa.html.

p. 65 For further reading on gender and sexual diversity, see, for example, these three accessible books by Meg-John Barker, illustrated by Jules Scheele (London: Icon Books): *Sexuality: A Graphic Guide* (2021); *Gender: A Graphic Guide* (2020); and *Queer: A Graphic History* (2016). See also Sam Killermann, *A Guide to Gender*, 2nd ed. (Austin: Impetus Books, 2017). For an online information and support space for LGBTQ youth, check out the Trevor Project, https://www.thetrevorproject.org/.

p. 80 As gender theorist Kate Bornstein writes, "Anyone who wants to question or study gender": Kate Bornstein, *My New Gender Workbook: A Step-by-Step Guide to Achieving World Peace through Gender Anarchy and Sex Positivity*, 2nd ed. (New York and London: Routledge, 2013), 126.

p. 85 Asexuality activist David Jay explains this point: David Jay, interview in "Everybody's *Not* Hooking Up: Asexuality on Campus and Beyond—Mark Carrigan Interviews David Jay," Shira Tarrant, ed. *Gender, Sex, and Politics: In the Street and Between the Sheets in the 21st Century* (New York: Routledge, 2016), 253, 257.

p. 87 "Students overestimate how much sex their peers are having": Lisa Wade, *American Hookup: The New Culture of Sex on Campus* (New York: Norton, 2017), 17.

p. 88 For further reading on asexuality, see, for example, CJ DeLuzio Chasin, "Reconsidering Asexuality and Its Radical Potential," *Feminist Studies* 39, no. 2 (2013): 405–26, www.jstor.org/stable/23719054; Karli June Cerankowski and Megan Milks, eds., *Asexualities: Feminist and Queer Perspectives* (New York: Routledge, 2014); Ela Przybyło, *Asexual Erotics: Intimate Readings of Compulsory Sexuality* (Columbus: Ohio State University Press, 2019). On a related topic of toxic cultural pressures and conventions around sexuality, see Rachel Hills, *The Sex Myth: The Gap between Our Fantasies and Reality* (New York: Simon & Schuster, 2015).

p. 88 For online information on asexuality organizations, see the Asexual Visibility and Education Network (AVEN), www.asexuality.org, and Asexual Outreach, https://aceweek.org.

Manisexto #3: Body Positivity

p. 95 The movement intersects powerfully with: For further reading about an intersectional approach to disability studies, see, for example, Alison Kafer, *Feminist, Queer, Crip* (Bloomington: Indiana University Press, 2013).

p. 99 One study found almost double the percentage of US women: Judy Kruger et al., "Body Size Satisfaction and Physical Activity Levels among Men and Women," *Obesity: A Research Journal* 16 (2008): 1976–79, doi.org/10.1038/oby.2008.311. See also Marisol Perez et al., "Body Dissatisfaction and Its Correlates in 5- to 7-Year-Old Girls: A Social Learning Experiment," *Journal of Clinical Child & Adolescent Psychology* 47, no. 5 (2018): 757–69, doi.org/10.1080/15374416.2016.1157758; Lauren Fiske et al., "Prevalence of Body Dissatisfaction among United States Adults: Review and Recommendations for Future Research," *Eating Behaviors* 15, no. 3 (2014): 357–65, doi.org/10.1016/j.eatbeh.2014.04.010; Hannah Quittkat et al., "Body Dissatisfaction, Importance of Appearance, and Body Appreciation in Men and Women over the Lifespan," *Frontiers in Psychiatry* 10 (Dec. 2019): art.864, doi.org/10.3389/fpsyt.2019.00864.

p. 100 "Of all the maddening side effects of our narrow cultural beauty standard": Kate Harding, "How Do You Fuck a Fat Woman?" in Jaclyn Friedman and Jessica Valenti, *Yes Means Yes!: Visions of Female Sexual Power & A World Without Rape* (Berkeley, CA: Seal Press, 2008), 72. See also, by Kate Harding and Marianne Kirby, *Lessons from the Fat-o-sphere: Quit Dieting and Declare a Truce with Your Body* (New York: Penguin, 2009).

p. 105 In 1967, a group of activists staged: "Curves Have Their Day in Park; 500 at a 'Fat-in' Call for Obesity," *New York Times*, June 5, 1967, 54, www .nytimes.com/1967/06/05/archives/curves-have-their-day-in-park-500-at-a -fatin-call-for-obesity.html.

p. 107 Users dub this online space the "Fatosphere": See, for example, Marissa Dickins et al., "The Role of the Fatosphere in Fat Adults' Responses to Obesity Stigma: A Model of Empowerment without a Focus on Weight Loss," *Qualitative Health Research* 21, no. 12 (2011): 1679–91, doi.org/10.1177 /1049732311417728; Marissa Dickins et al., "Social Inclusion and the Fatosphere: The Role of an Online Weblogging Community in Fostering Social Inclusion," *Sociology of Health and Illness* 38, no. 5 (2016): 797–811, doi.org /10.1111/1467-9566.12397.

p. 108 Researchers term the internalized desire to build muscle mass: See, for example, Jason M. Nagata et al., "Boys, Bulk, and Body Ideals: Sex Differences in Weight-Gain Attempts among Adolescents in the United States," *Journal of Adolescent Health* 64, no. 4 (2019): 450–53, doi.org/10.1016/j .jadohealth.2018.09.002; Jason M. Nagata et al., "Predictors of Muscularity-Oriented Disordered Eating Behaviors in U.S. Young Adults: A Prospective Cohort Study," *International Journal of Eating Disorders* 52, no. 12 (2019): 1380–88, doi.org/10.1002/eat.23094; Jason M. Lavender et al., "Men, Muscles, and Eating Disorders: An Overview of Traditional and Muscularity-Oriented Disordered Eating," *Current Psychiatry Reports* 19, no. 6 (2017): art.32, doi.org/10.1007/s11920-017-0787-5; Timothy Baghurst et al., "Change in Sociocultural Ideal Male Physique: An Examination of Past and Present Action Figures," *Body Image* 3, no. 1 (2006): 87–91, doi.org/10.1016/j.bodyim .2005.11.001.

p. 109 For further reading in the popular press about men's body image, see, for example, Sirin Kale, "Gym, Eat, Repeat: The Shocking Rise of Muscle Dysmorphia," *Guardian*, July 17, 2019, www.theguardian.com/lifeandstyle /2019/jul/17/gym-eat-repeat-the-shocking-rise-of-muscle-dysmorphia; Jerry Kennard, "Bigorexia or Muscle Dysmorphia," VeryWellMind.com, Nov. 21, 2020, www.verywellmind.com/bigorexia-muscular-dysmorphia -reverse-anorexia-2328475#citation-2.

p. 110 A related initiative is promoted: Linda Bacon, *Health at Every Size: The Surprising Truth about Your Weight* (Dallas: BenBella Books, 2010). For further reading about healthy body image and weight, see, for example, "Body Image," Office on Women's Health, US Department of Health & Human Services, March 27, 2019, www.womenshealth.gov/mental-health/body -image-and-mental-health/body-image#13, and "Size Diversity and Health at Every Size," by the National Eating Disorders Association, www

.nationaleatingdisorders.org/size-diversity-health-every-size. See also the Association for Size Diversity and Health (ASDAH), https://asdah.org/.

p. 115 The one item that sold well: Irina Aleksander, "Sweatpants Forever," *New York Times Magazine*, Aug. 9, 2020, 30.

p. 116 In fact, one recent study found that 90 percent of young women: Rosalind Gill, "Changing the Perfect Picture: Smartphones, Social Media, and Appearance Pressures," University of London, Gender and Sexualities Research Centre, 2021, www.city.ac.uk/__data/assets/pdf_file/0005/597209/Parliament-Report-web.pdf. For further reading, see also Sarah Fielding, "90% of Women Report Using a Filter on Their Photos," VeryWellMind.com, March 15, 2021, www.verywellmind.com/90-of-women-report-using-a-filter-on-their-photos-5116048#citation-1.

p. 117 Social media can, again, be part of both the problem and the solution: See, for example, Ellen Laan et al., "Young Women's Genital Self-Image and Effects of Exposure to Pictures of Natural Vulvas," *Journal of Psychosomatic Obstetrics & Gynecology* 38, no. 4 (2017): 249–55, DOI: 10.1080/0167482X.2016.1233172.

pp. 117–118 For further reading about circumcision and the intactivist movement, see, for example, Intact America, https://intactamerica.org/, and Brian J. Morris et al., "Estimation of Country-Specific and Global Prevalence of Male Circumcision," *Population Health Metrics* 14, no. 4 (2016), doi.org/10.1186/s12963-016-0073-5. For period positivity, see, for example, the work of the organization Period Positive, https://periodpositive.com/; Jennifer Weiss-Wolf's *Periods Gone Public: Taking a Stand for Menstrual Equity* (New York: Arcade Publishing, 2019); Nadya Okamoto, *Period Power: A Manifesto for the Menstrual Movement* (New York: Simon & Schuster, 2018); and Camilla Mørk Røstvik, *Cash Flow: The Businesses of Menstruation* (London: UCL Press, 2022).

p. 118 For the body-positive work of artist Jamie McCartney, see his websites The Great Wall of Vagina, https://jamiemccartney.com/portfolio/the-great-wall-of-vagina/, and Genital Art, https://jamiemccartney.com/genital-art/.

p. 119 The American Society of Aesthetic Plastic Surgeons reports: Rhett N. Willis et al., "Labiaplasty Minora Reduction," US National Library of Medicine, StatPearls Publishing, Nov. 2, 2021, www.ncbi.nlm.nih.gov/books/NBK448086/.

p. 122 For further reading about genital integrity, see, for example, Genital Autonomy America, https://www.gaamerica.org/, and the United Nations campaign "Free and Equal," https://www.unfe.org/intersex-awareness/.

p. 123 For further reading about body neutrality and confidence culture, see, for example, Anna Kessel, "The Rise of the Body Neutrality Movement: 'If

You're Fat, You Don't Have to Hate Yourself,'" *Guardian*, July 23, 2018, www
.theguardian.com/lifeandstyle/2018/jul/23/the-rise-of-the-body-neutrality
-movement-if-youre-fat-you-dont-have-to-hate-yourself; Shani Orgad and
Rosalind Gill, *Confidence Culture* (Durham, NC: Duke University Press,
2022).

p. 127   Many companies in the industries of fashion retail and personal grooming products: See, for example, "Be Real: The Campaign for Body Confidence," Dove, May 19, 2020, www.dove.com/uk/dove-self-esteem-project
/help-for-parents/talking-about-appearance/be-real-the-campaign-for
-body-confidence.html; Angela Celebre and Ashley Waggoner Denton, "The
Good, the Bad, and the Ugly of the Dove Campaign for Real Beauty," *The In-
quisitive Mind* 19 (2014), www.in-mind.org/article/the-good-the-bad-and
-the-ugly-of-the-dove-campaign-for-real-beauty; Aliza Pelto, "New #Aerie-
Real Role Models Represent Body Positivity in Fashion at Its Finest," *Bust*,
https://bust.com/style/196849-new-body-positive-american-eagle
-campaign.html; Seth McBride, "Aerie Steps Up Inclusive Advertising with
Wheelchair-Using Underwear Model," *New Mobility*, July 30, 2018, www
.newmobility.com/2018/07/aerie-inclusive-advertising/.

p. 128   Attention grabbing also are campaigns that switch the gender messaging onto men: See, for example, Dianna Christe, "Hanes Pushes Body Positivity in 'Every Bod' Campaign," *Marketing Dive*, Aug. 7, 2019, www
.marketingdive.com/news/hanes-pushes-body-positivity-in-every-bod
-campaign/560403/; "Surging Ahead: New Underwear Brand Surge Says
'Pants' to Male Body Image Issues and Uses Models of All Shapes and
Sizes," *Sun*, Aug. 10, 2018, www.thesun.co.uk/news/6983167/new-underwear
-brand-surge-says-pants-to-male-body-image-issues/.

p. 128   The body positive trend has become so pronounced: See, for example,
Seth Stevenson, "Victoria's Secret Has Only Itself to Blame," *Slate*, June 9,
2020, https://slate.com/business/2020/06/victoria-secret-coronavirus
-jeffrey-epstein-les-wexner.html; Sapna Maheshwari and Vanessa Friedman, "Victoria's Secret Swaps Angels for 'What Women Want.' Will They
Buy It?" *New York Times*, June 16, 2021, www.nytimes.com/2021/06/16
/business/victorias-secret-collective-megan-rapinoe.html; Lily Harrison,
"Lane Bryant Throws Shade at Victoria's Secret in New Sexy Lingerie Ad Titled '#ImNoAngel,'" *E! News*, April 7, 2015, www.eonline.com/news/643459
/lane-bryant-throws-shade-at-victoria-s-secret-in-new-sexy-lingerie-ad
-titled-imnoangel; Rowena Lindsay, "What's Behind the #ImNoAngel
Beauty Campaign?" *Christian Science Monitor*, April 7, 2015, www.csmonitor
.com/The-Culture/2015/0407/What-s-behind-the-ImNoAngel-beauty
-campaign.

p. 129 It is, however, this very success of body positivity that causes concern: See, for example, Stephanie Yeboah, "Why the Body Positivity Movement Still Has a Long Way to Go," *Vogue India*, May 29, 2020, www.vogue.in /wellness/content/body-positivity-fat-acceptance-movement-still-has-a -long-way-to-go.

Manisexto #4: Consent

pp. 139–140 One infamous example was: Chanel Miller, *Know My Name: A Memoir* (New York: Penguin, 2020).

p. 142 For further reading about campus sexual assault, see, for example, Jennifer S. Hirsch and Shamus Khan, *Sexual Citizens: A Landmark Study of Sex, Power, and Assault on Campus* (New York: Norton, 2020); Donna Freitas, *Consent on Campus: A Manifesto* (New York: Oxford University Press, 2018).

p. 145 Sex—and sexual consent—is not green eggs and ham: For a similar argument, see Rebecca Koon, "Consent and Green Eggs and Ham," *Outspoken Sex Ed*, March 2, 2022, www.outspokeneducation.com/post/consent-and -green-eggs-and-ham.

p. 152 This new and deeper understanding of consent: For two other takes on the concept of consent, see Joseph J. Fischel, *Screw Consent: A Better Politics of Sexual Justice* (Berkeley: University of California Press, 2019), and Christine Emba, *Rethinking Sex: A Provocation* (New York: Sentinel, 2022).

p. 163 The phrase "rape culture" refers to the normalization of sexual violence: For further reading, see, for example, Kate Harding, *Asking for It: The Alarming Rise of Rape Culture—And What We Can Do about It* (New York: Perseus Books/DaCapo, 2015); Roxane Gay, ed., *Not That Bad: Dispatches from Rape Culture* (New York: Harper, 2018).

p. 164 According to the National Sexual Violence Resource Center: "Statistics," National Sexual Violence Resource Center, www.nsvrc.org/statistics; "The Criminal Justice System: Statistics," Rape, Abuse & Incest National Network (RAINN), www.rainn.org/statistics/criminal-justice-system.

p. 165 In 2018, the American Psychological Association took on this issue: American Psychological Association, Boys and Men Guidelines Group, *APA Guidelines for Psychological Practice with Boys and Men*, 2018, www.apa.org /about/policy/psychological-practice-boys-men-guidelines.pdf.

p. 166 Promoting Healthy Manhood: Brian Heilman et al., "The Man Box: A Study on Being a Young Man in the US, UK, and Mexico," Washington DC and London: Promundo-US and Unilever, 2017, www.promundoglobal.org /resources/man-box-study-young-man-us-uk-mexico/?lang=english; "Men

Scoring Higher on 'Man Box' Scale Are Prone to Violence, Mental Illness," Promundo, Aug. 6, 2020, https://promundoglobal.org/men-scoring-higher -on-man-box-scale-are-prone-to-violence-mental-illness/#. For organiza- tions focused on healthy masculinity, see, for example, A Call to Men: The Next Generation of Manhood, www.acalltomen.org; Heads Up Guys (about depression among men), www.headsupguys.org; and Promundo: Healthy Masculinity, Gender Equality, https://promundoglobal.org/. For further reading about healthy masculinity, see, for example, Jackson Katz, *The Ma- cho Paradox: Why Some Men Hurt Women and How All Men Can Help*, revised ed. (Naperville, IL: Sourcebooks, 2019); Don McPherson, *You Throw Like a Girl: The Blind Spot of Masculinity* (New York: Edge of Sports, 2019); Ronald F. Levant and Shana Pryor, *The Tough Standard: The Hard Truths about Mas- culinity and Violence* (Oxford: Oxford University Press, 2020); Thomas Keith, *The Bro Code: The Fallout of Raising Boys to Objectify and Subordinate Women* (New York: Routledge, 2021); Tony Porter, *Breaking Out of the "Man Box": The Next Generation of Manhood* (New York: Skyhorse Publishing, 2021).

Manisexto #5: Shared Pleasure

p. 180 In terms of *power with* instead of *power over*: See, for example, Pamela Pansardi and Marianna Bindi, "The New Concepts of Power? Power-Over, Power-To and Power-With," *Journal of Political Power* 14, no. 1 (2021): 51–71, doi.org/10.1080/2158379X.2021.1877001.

p. 180 This problem of power-over relationships aligns with the problem of patriarchy: See, for example, Allan G. Johnson, *The Gender Knot: Unravel- ing Our Patriarchal Legacy*, 3rd ed. (Philadelphia: Temple University Press, 2014).

p. 183 To mention three very different examples: Immanuel Kant, *Groundwork of the Metaphysics of Morals* (1785). bell hooks, "Love as the Practice of Free- dom," in *Outlaw Culture: Resisting Representations* (New York: Routledge, 2006), 298; see also hooks, *All About Love: New Visions* (New York: William Morrow, 2000). Martin Buber, *I and Thou*, translated by Walter Kaufman (New York: Simon & Schuster, 1970).

p. 186 A word also about orgasm: For further reading in scholarship about orgasm, see, for example, Robert Muchembled, *Orgasm and the West: A His- tory of Pleasure from the Sixteenth Century to the Present*, translated by Jean Birrell (Cambridge, MA: Polity Press, 2008); Elisabeth A. Lloyd, *The Case of the Female Orgasm: Bias in the Science of Evolution* (Cambridge: Harvard Uni- versity Press, 2006).

p. 187 The goal, as sociologist of hookup culture Dr. Lisa Wade puts it: Lisa Wade, *American Hookup: The New Culture of Sex on Campus* (New York: Norton, 2017), 25.

p. 200 For further reading related to gender norms and equitable erotic pleasure, see, for example, adrienne maree brown, *Pleasure Activism: The Politics of Feeling Good* (Chico, CA, and Edinburgh: AK Press, 2019); Amia Srinivasan, *The Right to Sex: Feminism in the Twenty-First Century* (New York: Farrar, Straus and Giroux, 2021); Katherine Angel, *Tomorrow Sex Will Be Good Again: Women and Desire in the Age of Consent* (London: Verso, 2021).

pp. 203–204 As sociologist Lisa Wade reports: Lisa Wade, *American Hookup: The New Culture of Sex on Campus* (New York: Norton, 2017), 159.

p. 204 Learn more about the orgasm gap: Wade, "Unequal Pleasures," in *American Hookup*; Elisabeth A. Lloyd, *The Case of the Female Orgasm: Bias in the Science of Evolution* (Cambridge: Harvard University Press, 2006).

p. 205 Such pornography is not all bad: For further reading about "pornification" of the culture, see, for example, Kaarina Nikunen et al., eds., *Pornification: Sex and Sexuality in Media Culture* (London: Bloomsbury, 2007); Fiona Attwood, ed., *Mainstreaming Sex: The Sexualization of Western Culture* (London: I.B. Tauris, 2009); Brian McNair, *Porno? Chic! How Pornography Changed the World and Made It a Better Place* (London: Routledge, 2012); Eric Schaefer, ed., *Sex Scene: Media and the Sexual Revolution* (Durham, NC: Duke University Press, 2014).

p. 206 There's a convincing movement of feminist, queer, and ethical porn: Annie Sprinkle, *Hardcore from the Heart: The Pleasures, Profits and Politics of Sex in Performance* (New York: Continuum, 2001), 81. See also Tristan Taormino et al., eds., *The Feminist Porn Book: The Politics of Producing Pleasure* (New York: The Feminist Press at the City University of New York, 2013).

p. 206 Porn literacy: For two current examples of porn literacy programs, see the Boston Public Health Commission porn literacy curriculum, www.bphc .org/whatwedo/violence-prevention/start-strong/Pages/Porn-Literacy .aspx (featured in the *New York Times*), and the Toronto Teen Health Source (https://teenhealthsource.com/sex/porn-literacy/).

p. 208 "Young women have embraced this new reality": Lisa Wade, *American Hookup: The New Culture of Sex on Campus* (New York: Norton, 2017), 70.

p. 211 "The question to me, then, became less about whether hookups were 'good' or 'bad'": Peggy Orenstein, *Girls & Sex: Navigating the Complicated New Landscape* (New York: Harper, 2016), 111–12.

p. 214 According to numerous science-based studies: S. E. Stiritz, "Cultural Cliteracy: Exposing the Contexts of Women's Not Coming," *Berkeley Journal of Gender, Law & Justice* 23 (2008): 242–66; Laurie Mintz, *Becoming Cliterate:*

Why Orgasm Equality Matters—And How to Get It (New York: Harper, 2017); Lisa Wade, "Unequal Pleasures," in *American Hookup: The New Culture of Sex on Campus* (New York: Norton, 2017); Emily Nagoski, *Come As You Are: The Surprising New Science That Will Transform Your Sex Life*, revised ed. (New York: Simon & Schuster, 2021); Sarah Chadwick, *The Sweetness of Venus: A History of the Clitoris* (Boulder, CO: Armin Lear Press, 2021). See also *The Clitoris Journal: Multimedia Musings on All Things Clitoris*, https://clitoris.io /journal. See also adrienne maree brown, *Pleasure Activism: The Politics of Feeling Good* (Chico, CA, and Edinburgh: AK Press, 2019).

p. 214 "The clitoris really is the hokey pokey": Emily Nagoski, "Vaginas of Science, Vaginas of Justice: Representations of Healthy Female Sexual Functioning in Feminist Porn," *The Dirty Normal: Better Sex, Powered by Science*, April 6, 2013, www.thedirtynormal.com/2013/04/06/vaginas-of-science -vaginas-of-justice-representations-of-healthy-female-sexual-functioning -in-feminist-porn/.

p. 215 There's even a slang acronym for it: PIVMO: The term, in the somewhat different form of "Penile Intromission into the Vagina with Male Orgasm," was apparently coined by philosopher Kathryn Pauly Morgan. See Ronald B. de Sousa and Kathryn Pauly Morgan, "Philosophy, Sex and Feminism," *Atlantis, A Journal of Women's Studies* 13, no. 2 (1988), 3.

p. 217 The work of conceptual artist Sophia Wallace: Sophia Wallace, *Cliteracy: 100 Natural Laws*, 2012, www.sophiawallace.art/works#/cliteracy-100 -natural-laws/ and www.sophiawallace.art/works. See also Wallace's TED talk, "A Case for Cliteracy," Oct. 2014, www.ted.com/talks/sophia_wallace _a_case_for_cliteracy?language=en.

p. 219 For further reading about female genital cutting or mutilation, see the World Health Organization (WHO), www.who.int/health-topics/female -genital-mutilation#tab=tab_1, and the Orchid Project, www.orchidproject .org/.

p. 221 As the coeditors of *The Feminist Porn Book* note: Tristan Taormino et al., eds., *The Feminist Porn Book: The Politics of Producing Pleasure* (New York: The Feminist Press at the City University of New York, 2013), 14. Sarah MacLean, "Why Bashing Romance Novels Is Slut-Shaming," *Bustle*, Sept. 29, 2016, www.bustle.com/articles/186881-sarah-maclean-bashing-romance -novels-is-just-another-form-of-slut-shaming. For further reading about woman-oriented erotica and romance fiction, see, for example, Clarissa Smith, *One for the Girls! The Pleasures and Practices of Reading Women's Porn* (Bristol, UK: Intellect Books, 2007); Catherine M. Roach, *Happily Ever After: The Romance Story in Popular Culture* (Bloomington: Indiana University

Press, 2016); Jayashree Kamblé et al., eds., *The Routledge Research Companion to Popular Romance Fiction* (New York: Routledge, 2020).

p. 226 Cultural scripts about appropriate sexuality and gender norms intertwine: For further reading about the narrative/imperative of romantic love in American culture and commerce, see, for example, Chrys Ingraham, *White Weddings: Romancing Heterosexuality in Popular Culture* (New York: Routledge, 1999); Catherine M. Roach, *Happily Ever After: The Romance Story in Popular Culture* (Bloomington: Indiana University Press, 2016); Laurie Essig, *Love, Inc. Dating Apps, the Big White Wedding, and Chasing the Happily Neverafter* (Oakland: University of California Press, 2019).

p. 229 In a groundbreaking essay entitled "Thinking Sex": Gayle S. Rubin, "Thinking Sex: Notes for a Radical Theory of the Politics of Sexuality," in Carole S. Vance, ed., *Pleasure and Danger: Exploring Female Sexuality* (Boston: Routledge & Kegan Paul, 1984), 267–319. See also Rubin's more recent reflections on her original essay: Gayle Rubin, "Blood Under the Bridge: Reflections on 'Thinking Sex,'" *GLQ: A Journal of Lesbian and Gay Studies* 17, no. 1 (2011): 15–48, doi.org/10.1215/10642684-2010-015.

p. 231 Society is increasingly thinking outside the couple norm: For further reading, see, for example, Eric Klinenberg, *Going Solo: The Extraordinary Rise and Surprising Appeal of Living Alone* (New York: Penguin, 2012); Kate Bolick, *Spinster: Making a Life of One's Own* (New York: Penguin Random House, 2015); Bella DePaulo, *How We Live Now: Redefining Home and Family in the 21st Century* (New York: Simon & Schuster, 2015); Rebecca Traister, *All the Single Ladies: Unmarried Women and the Rise of an Independent Nation* (New York: Simon & Schuster, 2016); Sasha Roseneil et al., *The Tenacity of the Couple-Norm: Intimate Citizenship Regimes in a Changing Europe* (London: UCL Press, 2020). For more on consensual nonmonogamy, see, for example, Janet W. Hardy and Dossie Easton, *The Ethical Slut: A Practical Guide to Polyamory, Open Relationships, and Other Freedoms in Sex and Love*, 3rd ed. (Berkeley, CA: Ten Speed Press, 2017).

p. 232 These practices were acknowledged: American Dialect Society, "2019 Word of the Year Is '(My) Pronouns,' Word of the Decade Is Singular 'They,'" Jan. 3, 2020, https://www.americandialect.org/2019-word-of-the-year-is-my-pronouns-word-of-the-decade-is-singular-they. For more on International Pronouns Day, see the website https://pronounsday.org/.

Afterglow: Where We Go from Here

p. 237 Almost half of all pregnancies in the US are unintended: Guttmacher Institute, "Unintended Pregnancy in the United States," Jan. 2019, www .guttmacher.org/fact-sheet/unintended-pregnancy-united-states.

p. 238 Of all areas of public policy, sexuality education is the most neglected: United Nations Youth, "Youth and Comprehensive Sexuality Education Fact Sheet," www.un.org/esa/socdev/documents/youth/fact-sheets/youth -sexuality-education.pdf; Guttmacher Institute, "Sex and HIV Education," March 1, 2022, www.guttmacher.org/state-policy/explore/sex-and-hiv -education; Centers for Disease Control and Prevention, "What Works: Sexual Health Education," www.cdc.gov/healthyyouth/whatworks/what-works -sexual-health-education.htm.

p. 239 #GenerationEquality: United Nations Population Fund, *The Journey towards Comprehensive Sexuality Education—Global Status Report*, Nov. 3, 2021, www.unfpa.org/publications/journey-towards-comprehensive-sexuality -education-global-status-report; United Nations Women, "Generation Equality: Realizing Women's Rights for an Equal Future," www.unwomen .org/en/get-involved/beijing-plus-25.

p. 241 Check out these education models for supporting healthy sexual citizenship: (1) Unitarian Universalist Association, Our Whole Lives (OWL) Lifespan Sexuality Education, www.uua.org/re/owl; (2) Amy T. Schalet's ABCD (autonomy, building healthy relationships, connectedness, diversity) model, www.amyschalet.com/resources/; see also her article "The New ABCD's of Talking about Sex with Teenagers," *HuffPost*, Jan. 2, 2012, www.huffpost. com/entry/teenagers-sex-talk_b_1072504, and her book *Not under My Roof: Parents, Teens, and the Culture of Sex* (Chicago: University of Chicago Press, 2011); (3) Centers for Disease Control and Prevention, *Adolescent Health: What Works in Schools*, www.cdc.gov/healthyyouth/whatworks/index.htm; (4) The United Nations Population Fund, *International Technical Guidance on Sexuality Education: An Evidence-Informed Approach*, revised ed., 2018, www .unfpa.org/publications/international-technical-guidance-sexuality -education; (5) AMAZE, online sex education, https://amaze.org/.

p. 241 Decades of research on successful models of education confirm: Eva S. Goldfarb and Lisa D. Lieberman, "Three Decades of Research: The Case for Comprehensive Sex Education," *Journal of Adolescent Health* 68, no. 1 (2021): 13–27, doi.org/10.1016/j.jadohealth.2020.07.036; Peggy Orenstein, *Girls & Sex: Navigating the Complicated New Landscape* (New York: Harper, 2016), 211. For further reading about purity culture and alternatives within Christianity, see, for example, Linda Kay Klein, *Pure: Inside the Evangelical Move-*

ment That Shamed a Generation of Young Women and How I Broke Free (New York: Atria, 2018), and Nadia Bolz-Weber, *Shameless: A Sexual Reformation* (New York: Convergent, 2019).

p. 242 Good sex ed supports: Eva S. Goldfarb and Lisa D. Lieberman, "Three Decades of Research: The Case for Comprehensive Sex Education," *Journal of Adolescent Health* 68, no. 1 (2021): 13–27, doi.org/10.1016/j.jadohealth.2020 .07.036.

p. 244 The Human Rights Campaign reports: Human Rights Campaign, *An Epidemic of Violence: Fatal Violence against Transgender and Gender Nonconforming People in the United States in 2021,* https://reports.hrc.org/an -epidemic-of-violence-fatal-violence-against-transgender-and-gender-non -confirming-people-in-the-united-states-in-2021.

p. 244 This Gen Z demographic provides the clearest window on America at the tipping point: Justin McCarthy, "U.S. Support for Gay Marriage Stable, at 63%" Gallup, May 22, 2019, https://news.gallup.com/poll/257705/support -gay-marriage-stable.aspx; Jeffrey M. Jones, "LGBT Identification Rises to 5.6% in Latest U.S. Estimate," Gallup, Feb. 24, 2021, https://news.gallup.com /poll/329708/lgbt-identification-rises-latest-estimate.aspx.

INDEX

CATHERINE M. ROACH

has twenty-five years of grant-funded research experience on gender, sexuality, and American popular culture. A two-time Fulbright awardee with a PhD from Harvard and publications in both fiction and nonfiction, she's been an invited visiting professor in Canada, Australia, and Europe. She is Professor of New College, an innovative liberal arts program at the University of Alabama, where she's won the school's top research and teaching awards and where she offers a popular cross-university course titled Sexuality & Society. Originally from Ottawa, Canada, she is based in Tuscaloosa, Alabama.